DAVID PAGE COFFIN

Sewing Shirts
with a Perfect Fit

The Ultimate Guide to Fit, Style, and Construction
from Collared and Cuffed to Blouses and Tunics

Includes
Basic Patterns for Sizes
from XXXS to XXXL

Learn to Work with Any
Body Shape

Achieve a Loose, Fitted,
or Tight Fit and Style in
Multiple Ways

QUARRY

Brimming with creative inspiration, how-to projects, and useful information to enrich your everyday life, Quarto Knows is a favorite destination for those pursuing their interests and passions. Visit our site and dig deeper with our books into your area of interest: Quarto Creates, Quarto Cooks, Quarto Homes, Quarto Lives, Quarto Drives, Quarto Explores, Quarto Gifts, or Quarto Kids.

First Published in 2018 by Quarry Books, an imprint of The Quarto Group, 100 Cummings Center, Suite 265-D, Beverly, MA 01915, USA. T (978) 282-9590 F (978) 283-2742 QuartoKnows.com

Quarry Books titles are also available at discount for retail, wholesale, promotional, and bulk purchase. For details, contact the Special Sales Manager by email at specialsales@quarto.com or by mail at The Quarto Group, Attn: Special Sales Manager, 401 Second Avenue North, Suite 310, Minneapolis, MN 55401, USA.

10 9 8 7 6 5 4 3 2 1

ISBN: 978-1-58923-952-4

Digital edition published in 2019

Library of Congress Cataloging-in-Publication Data
Names: Coffin, David Page, author.
Title: Sewing shirts for a perfect fit : the ultimate guide to fit, style, and construction from collared and cuffed to blouses and tunics / David Coffin.
Description: Beverly, MA, USA : Quarry Books, an imprint of The Quarto Group, 2019.
Identifiers: LCCN 2018035738 | ISBN 9781589239524 (trade pbk.)
Subjects: LCSH: Shirts, Men's. | Blouses. | Dressmaking.
Classification: LCC TT612 .C638 2019 | DDC 646.4/02--dc23 LC record available at https://lccn.loc.gov/2018035738

Design and Page Layout: Megan Jones Design
Photography: David Coffin, except pages 5, 8, 9, 10, 11, 12, 22, 23, 118, 119 (top left) are shutterstock
Illustration: David Coffin

Printed in China

To my incomparable mother, Elizabeth Gring Coffin, whose insistence that I take over the ironing of my own shirts in high school, when I started to get picky about the details, surely started something that neither of us could see at the time but has turned out very well. Thanks for that—love you always, Mom!

CONTENTS

FIT | 5

DRAPING THE TIGHT SHIRT 76

SEW | PROJECTS

BASIC SHIRT CONSTRUCTION 88

INTRODUCTION

WHAT THIS BOOK IS ABOUT AND WHAT IT ISN'T

This book is to guide home sewists, of all sewing and patternmaking skills, in the development of unique, personal, and well-fitted basic shirt patterns for themselves or anyone else, male and female, any shape, any size. *Sewing Shirts with a Perfect Fit*, is organized in two parts: a draping/fitting section followed by a project-based sewing section.

Fitting My approach to creating these patterns doesn't start with choosing a commercial pattern, taking extensive body measurements, and poring over size charts. There are no flat-pattern alterations based on all these usual preparations, nor any lists of body-shape "issues" with associated pattern fixes. Nor will you find any directions for drafting a pattern based on body measurements and ease formulas. Instead, I'll show you how to create perfectly fitting patterns quickly and intuitively by manipulating fabric directly on a body or dress form until it drapes smoothly into the shape and fit of the shirt you want to make, with no obvious wrinkles or grain distortions.

The draping portion of the book is divided into five chapters. Chapters 1 and 2 are big-picture overviews of shirt styles and fitting in general. The remaining three chapters explore achieving three specific types of shirt fit: loosely fitted, fitted, and tightly fitted (or very snug), using direct fabric manipulations on an actual body or torso form, in combination with pattern shapes from the included full-size pattern sheet. If you prefer, you can use the same pattern shapes from any standard commercial shirt pattern or copy them from a favorite existing shirt. It doesn't matter where the initial basic pattern pieces come from, the draping for perfect fit process is the same.

Sewing Once you've seen how a basic draping process works to create patterns, I'll walk you through four specific shirt-type example projects to demonstrate how on-the-spot draping can be incorporated into the construction process. This unique fitting process ensures an equally customized and perfected fit for each new shirt project you undertake. You can then adapt your carefully fitted patterns to design shirts for a wide range of different fabrics, new details, and even varying degrees of fitting ease.

The garment examples in the second section, demonstrate part of the range of possibilities any basic shirt pattern offers, and hopefully includes styles and features that many readers will find interesting. If I've not hit your particular interests with these examples, you might wish to check either of my two previous books on shirt making, both of which focus extensively on other detail and style options for shirt makers. Details from any commercial patterns can, of course, be added or adapted to make any well-fitting shirt style.

So that sewers at any experience level can follow along, additional information, beyond that which fits in the pages of this book, is available for download at www.quartoknows.com/page/sewing-shirts.com. The extra material covers in greater detail the basics of making muslin test garments to reshape existing flat patterns or to make new flat patterns from the draped pieces. It also includes more detailed step-by-step sewing steps, as you would find in a purchased pattern, for the sewing projects in the second section of this book.

WHY TRY DRAPING?

Many sewers, I'm guessing, when they hear the word "draping" immediately picture a designer standing before a model, lengths of uncut yardage in hand and pins gripped between lips, contemplating how next to astonish the world with some new fashion statement, arranging the fabric on the form like a florist would arrange a bouquet, for maximum freshness, impact, and style. This is *not* the sense in which I'll be using the term!

I persist in calling the process I'll be showing you "draping" because we will be pinning minimally cut fabric lengths on a form or model to create a pattern, but also because a more precise label—I'd prefer "fitting"—is already taken, or at least already comes laden with the sort of associations I mentioned previously. In other words, I will not be using all the typical flat-pattern manipulation fitting methods with which most home sewers are familiar.

Why skip these? Two reasons. First, they're already well described in many other books, while draping is not. More importantly, no matter which other methods might be used to arrive at a pattern that fits a specific body, eventually every pattern is tested in fabric (in muslin or not!) on that body. And unless that test proves 100% successful, some shifting and pinning of the fabric while directly on the person/form is necessary to achieve the desired result that measurements, flat-pattern tweaks, and pattern drafting approaches can only approximate. So, my approach is simply to skip all the preparatory steps and go right to adjusting fabric on the body/form. And then create the pattern from the draped fabric pieces that you know will fit perfectly.

It's my experience that, for shirts at least, it's quite easy and practical, and possibly much faster overall, even for beginners, to skip ahead to this "testing on the body" step. In effect, we'll be cutting to the chase by directly developing the core skill that all fitting ultimately rests upon, which is knowing how to respond when you see the draped and then stitched-together fabric peices doing something you don't want, or don't like, when it's on your body.

Of course, if you're already getting great fitting results using any other approach, I'm not suggesting that you "fix it" by switching over to what I'll show you here, but if you are struggling, this book offers another option. Countless interactions over the years, both as an instructor, and as a staff member at *Threads* magazine—situations in which one hears about the challenges every day sewers experience—have reinforced my own experiences fitting myself and others. Fitting is difficult! For many, I'll venture it's the most persistently challenging part of the entire garment-making process, despite much effort.

There's no shortage of books, articles, and classes on fitting, as there were when I was first struggling with fitting shirts on myself several decades ago. I certainly did try to find clear answers to the many specific issues I was baffled by . . . and did get some help. But, so often, the apparent solutions had unexplained limits (". . . add up to an inch . . ."?!) or would simply create different problems when a shifted seamline would clear up one wrinkle only to create new ones elsewhere. I remain amazed at the number of fitting texts I've searched that never even mention that basic shirt-related feature, the shoulder yoke, or offer any acknowledgment of the existence of asymmetric body parts—and those resources that do address asymmetric issues, uniformly suggest body padding to conceal differences, which is not a shirt-friendly solution.

Since many sewers, by definition, find themselves within the bell curve of typical body shapes, it's no surprise that their usual strategy for fitting themselves is to search for right-now spot fixes, rather than big-picture understanding. But it is normal and acceptable to have a body shape outside the comfortable confines of pretty much "average," as so many of us know all too well, even if we didn't even really notice this until we try to fit ourselves!

It's precisely those of us with more complex fitting issues that persist in looking for help, so it's largely with us in mind that I'm offering this not commonly used, back-to-first-principles draping method.

The downside to this drape-to-fit process, if not obvious already, is that it's tough to drape on oneself! This is the main reason for the vast prevalence of flat-pattern-altering approaches, as well as serious justification for the get-expert-help alternative, for those home-sewists who don't have a fitting partner or dress form. A customized, personal dress form—about which more later—will eventually prove essential if you're the fittee as well as fitter. But for now, if you're fitting others or have a potential fitting buddy, call them and propose a partnership!

FIT | 1
SHIRTS: AN OVERVIEW

WHAT'S A SHIRT?

Shirts (or "button-ups" as some readers may prefer) are upper-body garments that include the following construction characteristics:

1. A shirt is almost always cut from single layers of woven-fabric (sorry, knit shirts not covered here), except for common neck- and wrist-finishing details such as collars and cuffs, and closure-reinforcing bands, all of which may be cut from double fabric layers (or they are faced or folded back).

2. A shirt rarely has any sort of built-in body- or silhouette-shaping devices or layers, such as shoulder, chest, or bust pads; boning; or other stiffening. Areas such as cuffs and collars are commonly interfaced for the sake of preserving, smoothing, and emphasizing their own specific shape, not the body wearing the garment.

3. Quite commonly, but not necessarily, shirts are joined at the shoulders with another double-layered area called a yoke; double layers of a yoke help strengthen the shoulder area and provide an easy and non-chafing way to offset and finish the shoulder seams in a single-layer garment.

4. Usually a shirt is hemmed in such a nonobtrusive way that it can be either worn tucked into a waistband or left untucked.

5. Typically, shirts are made from basic pattern shapes that don't obviously mimic or attempt to follow body curves and contours and are, more often than not, intended to be worn loose rather than tight. This last characteristic is, of course, exactly what we'll be exploring in this book, and so the drape-to-fit process requires that, to some degree, we understand all the other elements that make a shirt a shirt, assuming we want our project to still be a shirt when we're finished.

BASIC SHIRT SHAPES: THE RECTANGULAR BODY

The vast majority of manufactured shirts have bodies just like those below, bodies that are basically rectangular, with fronts, which when closed are the same width as the backs. Additionally, these shirts are typically constructed with straight, on-grain side seams from the armholes to the hems, and the shoulder width at the top of the armholes is equal in width to the body or just a little smaller.

Shirt body shapes like this are clearly a sensible and practical choice for manufacturers because they keep patternmaking issues and sizing choices as simple as possible. They ensure that, no matter where the customer's upper body is widest—at the shoulders, chest, waist, or hips—as long as that width is less than the shirt body's uniform width anywhere, the shirt will be wearable . . . and most customers will think that it "fits" or at least fits as well as can be expected.

This same rectangular strategy has been used for literally thousands of years by makers and wearers of basic upper-body garments the world over and it helped create the ancestors of the modern shirt. This persistence is not about style or tradition as much as simple effectiveness. For much of our history as woven-fabric clothes-wearers, it was even more relentlessly applied, with the rectangle ruling every part and detail of many basic upper garments, as worn by people at every level of society. This approach also reduced any need for personalized garment shaping to the barest minimum, clearly a virtue when all woven-fabric garments were necessarily both hand-woven and hand-sewn, one at a time.

But it's not the history that interests me. Again, it's the sheer effectiveness of the rectangle as an upper-body garment shape, even when, as in those earlier epochs, the shoulders, sleeves, and armholes are also completely rectangular and curve free.

Look, below, how these completely rectangular-shouldered, traditional yet still contemporary garments manage to mold to the wearers shoulders quite well, despite their shape. This is due to the natural flexibility and weight—in other words, the drape—of the woven fabric. This may seem a minor detail compared to the obvious nonfitting excesses of fabric elsewhere in garments, but as we'll see next, this wide-shoulder solution is still very much in place on a huge proportion of existing, everyday, nontraditional shirts.

THE LOOSE SHIRT: NOT FITTED, BUT STILL FITS

We can be quite sure that none of the shirts pictured below are made entirely from rectangular pieces because they feature shoulders that are—to some degree—angled downward, with curved armholes and shaped sleeve caps. Like the modern shirts shown flat on the previous pages, note how they all have (as purely rectangular garments do) shoulder widths that are greater than their wearer's actual shoulders. And notice, in each case pictured here, how smoothly both the shirt shoulders (from the ends of the shoulders inward) and the fronts lay against the wearer's bodies, with all the excess shirt width falling to the sides and against the sleeves, which, in every case, are as loose fitting as the bodies from which they fall.

It's equally unlikely that any of these shirts have shoulder slopes that were custom fit to the bodies inside. In fact, what I gather from these examples, and the endless others I've seen walking around, is that when the garment shoulder on a loose and basically rectangular garment is wider than the body, it doesn't matter what the shoulder angle is, because the natural drape of the garment will simply adapt to the body shape, from shoulder to shoulder, so that the shirt falls smoothly over the body, because it's wide enough to do so. What happens under the arms and below the upper chest depends on the body shape beneath the garment, but if the overall width is sufficient to cover whatever is there without discomfort, the job is done for the loose shirt, no further fitting required.

The easy, practical magic and popularity of the basic, generic rectangular garment persists in shirts like these, and not just for powerless victims of manufacturing economies, but by choice as a desirable, natural looking, everyday style because of the completely nonbinding freedom of movement these garments still deliver.

Of course, as garment makers as well as wearers, we sewers are nonetheless very likely to want to improve the fit of any garments or patterns that fit like some these examples, which is what the rest of this book is about. I believe it's important to recognize that for many wearers, these loose examples are not examples of poor fit but are, in fact, good examples of exactly what makes some shirts, favorite shirts.

HERE'S ANOTHER WAY TO COMPARE THE PURELY RECTANGULAR SHIRT AND THE MODERN LOOSE SHIRT

The illustration, below left, shows the pure rectangle with a neck opening and armholes drawn in red; the illustration on the right shows the modern loose shirt. The modern loose shirt is shown with a rounded neck and curved and slightly dropped armholes. This significantly advances the cause of matching shirt shape to body shape, but these openings are no more personalized than those on the rectangular shirt. Nor are the shirt bodies really any different. Both have fronts and backs identical in width and alignment, and both place the shoulder, and thus the back neckline and the sleeve center lines, right at the top edge where the fronts and backs meet.

So, the placement of the openings is improved in the modern version, but the strategy for fitting the body of the wearer with either the rectangular or modern shirt body remains the same, which is about as sophisticated and personalized as a sandwich board, and will settle on any specific body (if an open collar allows), with little regard for the actual body shape within.

Remarkably enough, this often works out fairly well with shirts (they're woven fabric, which helps!), even though very few humans are the same width—or length—in the front and back, with shoulders perfectly symmetrical, and necks protruding at just the slightly forward-tilting angle that these necklines predict.

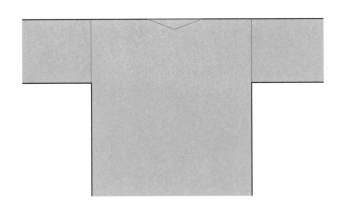

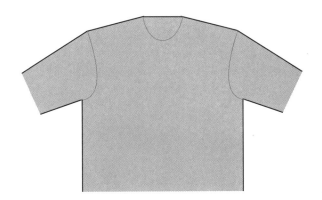

HOW DO SHIRTS FIT?

If a "well-fitting garment" is defined as one that covers the body smoothly, with few if any wrinkles when worn, woven-fabric shirts simply don't now, and never have, actually fit the definition. They've always been the garment equivalent of sheets on a bed with someone sleeping in it.

Nor have most shirts ever really been expected to fit any better than this, even now when the trend is for very tight fit. Compare the two upper rows of images, below,

of typical, classic shirt silhouettes, with the generally more current, modern examples in the two lower rows, and you'll see that shirt wrinkling gets more complex as shirt shapes get both less rectangular and smaller. Tighter clothes must deal with ever more complex body shapes and must be more uniquely fitted to benefit all the various types (and shapes) of unique bodies.

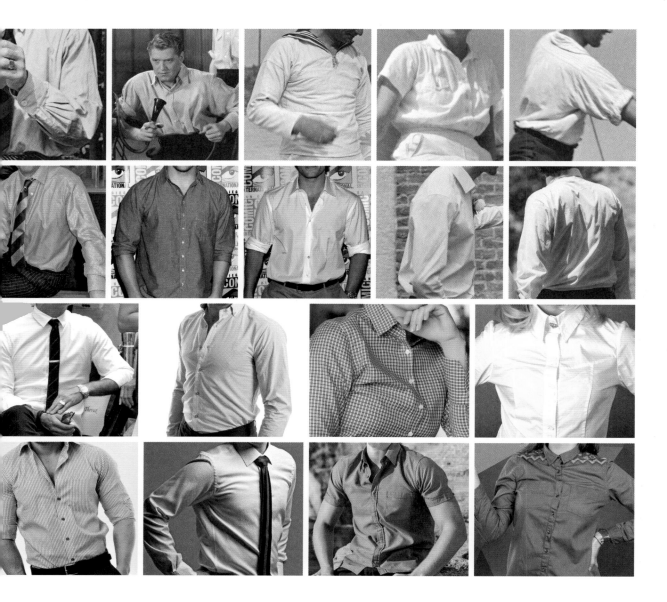

Because woven shirts are generally lightweight-fabric garments with no built-in shape support except the body it is covering, it's inevitable that shirts will wrinkle as a reaction to almost any movement of that body, so the most telling images on the previous pages are those in which the wearer is more or less standing still and upright, with arms down at the sides. If the shirt is straining, slumping, or otherwise wrinkling around even such a default position, we can't excuse these wrinkles as temporarily motion induced. Instead, we'll use these specific types of wrinkles as our guides to creating a better fit, and let the motion-induced wrinkles live on. However, we will remain alert to any options for reducing or adjusting motion-induced wrinkles if we feel compelled to do so, by wearing comfort, or for any other reason.

Put another way, I'll be confining my fitting goal in this book to this: To remove or reduce wrinkles on the torso form or on a standing-straight-and-still body as much as possible, as shown in examples below, while keeping the fabric grain as level and vertical as possible, all while adjusting the amount of ease through three different,

roughly defined levels of fit: loosely fitted, fitted, and tightly fitted. I'll leave any further pattern refinements up to each reader/maker/wearer, with particular regards toward comfort and planned activity levels.

Still, it's worth noting that there's quite a wide range of completely subjective things we might also mean when we think or feel that a shirt, or any garment, "fits" beyond not wrinkling when standing still.

- We could mean it's flattering, making the wearer look good, perhaps by revealing the figure inside to advantage, or by concealing it, or by doing a bit of both.

- Or we might mean that some certain style or fashionable silhouette has been well balanced with the shape of a unique body. This may require that the garment not match the body inside in some places or ways. Keep in mind though, that very few shirts will have been custom-fitted to the wearer, so very few styles of wearing them will be based on this option.

- Maybe we mean the garment feels good to wear: it's comfortable, regardless of how it may look, which is directly related to, and can vary considerably depending on, what activities we're engaging in while wearing it.

- Or we might mean that we feel good wearing it, which could be quite different for those who like a loose, nonbinding fit above all else and those who like tight and may even prefer some binding somewhere to feeling swamped or hidden in anything too loose.

For these, or any other subjective reasons, any of the shirt-wearers at left could reasonably feel that their shirt "fits" just as they prefer. But for our purposes, suffice it to say that a wrinkle-free start will probably be a useful one, and good to know how to achieve in any case.

Finally, it's important to realize that the more we reshape a generic, simple shirt to match our unique shape in one set position, the less easily it may sit on us as we take other positions, so we'll always have to test for good-fitting against overfitting.

FIT | 2
FITTING: THE BIG PICTURE

DRAPING MAGIC

Here, again, are the diagrams from page 11, comparing rectangular and modern shaped shirts with the armholes and necklines further simplified into three connected ovals, which I hope you can see captures the essence of the difference between the two garment shapes at the shoulders.

Now imagine that you could capture the exact positions and shapes of your own unique neckline and armhole ovals simply by dropping floating circles of magic string around each oval and shaping the magic string as you wish, and then freeze all the ovals in place, by flowing some other magic substance over them all, capturing both the overall shape of the shirt and the inner contours of the shoulders that connect the ovals and their exact distances and orientations from each other . . . and then, with a finger snap, convert all this to a flat pattern.

This is exactly what we are going do with this drape-to-fit technique I've been referring to, allowing the very real flexibilities of fabric itself provide all the magic we'll need. We'll do it in a different order, with no finger snapping (sorry!), but the result will be almost as magical, I think.

The real-world "magical object" we'll "float" onto our target body to locate the openings is a *yoke*. Think of the yoke as the fabric equivalent of the connected-ovals schematic for the shirt openings at right, as well as a fabric device for capturing the contours, widths, and orientations of the two shoulders in between the neckline and armhole ovals. So, our first step, described in detail on page 33, is to trace a yoke pattern, either from the included multisize pattern, or from a favorite commercial pattern, or even from a favorite shirt.

Once we have a fabric yoke, the contour of the actual back neckline determines how the fabric yoke is positioned initially on the body or on the torso form (no need for a center back measurement!). If the fabric yoke is cut wider than the body or torso form, you can easily

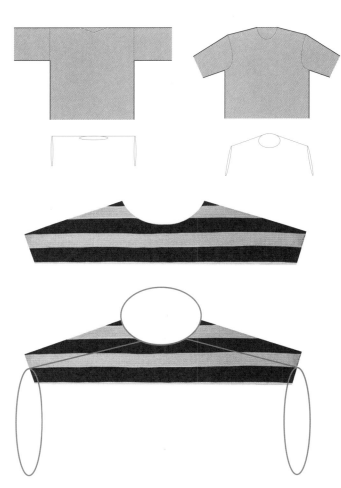

fold the ends under at the shoulder edges. Then you will record the shoulder lengths of the yoke on each side of the neck (which might possibly be asymmetrical measurements). And, in our floating example, we can then "float" the armholes at the exact ends of the shoulders, which means ultimately your shirt will have perfectly positioned armhole seams, with sleeves that hang from your exact shoulder points.

The "magic" for me starts with how this yoke, a completely abstract, symmetrical, geometrical, non-body-shaped, cut-out detail, can so easily and naturally mold itself to whatever shape it's laid upon, while remaining quite smooth and relaxed. Here's how the same yoke appears on six unique necks and shoulders. Each example shows how the yoke transforms without altering its pattern shape, except for a few straight folds, as needed to conform to the length and width of the actual body, along the edges of each shoulder and the front and back of the yoke.

AN "IN-A-NUTSHELL" INTRODUCTION TO MY DRAPE-TO-FIT PROCESS

Here's a quick outline of my basic shirt-draping process. The step-by-step details, applied to various body shapes with various levels of fitting ease, follow in subsequent chapters, in which you'll learn in detail, how to use the included multisize pattern as the source for your yoke pattern, front and back armhole-curve patterns, and a sleeve pattern with a cap length (the seam that gets sewn to the armhole) that matches the armhole curves.

1. Cut out the yoke, then position and mold it to a body or dress form as shown.

2. Next, cut two rectangles of gingham (the perfect draping fabric because its easy to see the fabric grain), each large enough to more than cover the front and the back of the body. For the front rectangle, guesstimate and mark a smallish neckline curve in the center. Drape the rectangles to fit the body or form front and back by placing the cut edges of the gingham pieces over and on top of the yoke. Pin both pieces to the yoke so the grain is perfectly vertical and square along all yoke edges. With permanent marking pen, mark the draped rectangles at the intersection of the yoke edges. Be sure to mark the shoulder ends of the yoke, too.

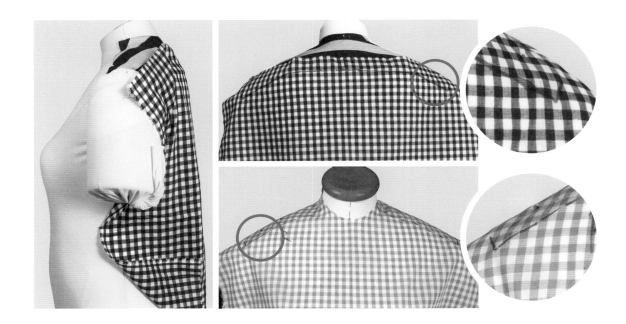

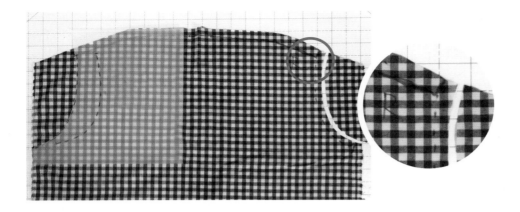

3. Remove the rectangles from the form or body. Allowing generous seam allowances, trim away the extra fabric along the markings.

4. Trace the armhole design lines (from the multisize pattern) onto the front and back rectangles at the yoke-end marks and trim, allowing generous seam allowances.

5. Draw side seams straight down from the bottom of each of the armhole markings. Next, baste the rectangles to the yoke as marked and close the side seams, then put the drape back on the form or body to adjust the angle of the side seams and evaluate the general fit.

6. In this example, there's a side-seam angle problem (because the front rectangle is shorter than the back one). By evenly folding out this excess across the back, we visually balance the front and back, but this also shortens the back armhole. But don't worry, if the armhole looks okay with the shortened length, as this one does, just leave everything alone or simply choose a different armhole design line or redraw the first armhole design line to return to the back armhole curve to its original length (more on this later).

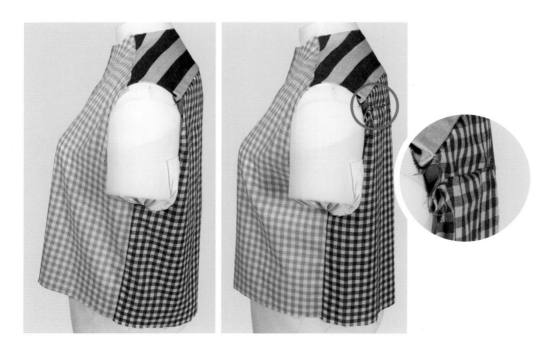

7. There seems clearly to be more fabric width in back than is needed or looks good, so I pinned it out vertically and then basted along the pin markings to reduce the width. The reduced armhole seemed to look good, so I measured the new length, and found a better-matching sleeve cap length from the multi-size pattern.

   The horizontal tuck across the back permanently changes the back pattern and disappears into it, while the vertical ones at the back waist can become darts, or be converted to seams, or even be used to permanently reshape the side seams, as you'll see later.

8. Next, stitch up a test sleeve and baste it into the armhole curve. In this example, the sleeve is straining against the arm, so it'll be a good idea to check the real body this form represents.

9. I like to use a paper strip to represent any number of different neckline design lines. This shows a collar on a stand, but many other style lines are as easy to sketch on paper or directly on the fabric with a marker.

So, in just these few steps we've draped our way to a complete and fully customized basic shirt muslin. By tracing the marked seams from this to paper, we can easily create a pattern from it (see "Pin- and Wheel-Tracing," pages 26–27, and the additional online material).

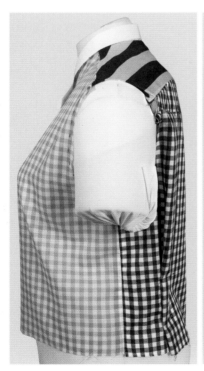

USING THE PROVIDED MULTISIZE PATTERN; WHERE'S THE BODY?

As my nutshell explanation proves, you can create a full test muslin with almost no measuring and no paper-pattern manipulation. And to do this, we needed only three pattern pieces, or more accurately, one piece (a yoke) and three seam line shapes (two armhole curves and one matching sleeve cap). Since these are provided in this book's full-size pattern collection, shown below, you're good to go! And since yokes and curves are also provided in many millions of existing multisized shirt patterns or can be pin-traced from any comfortable

shirt already hanging in your own closet, you have many options.

Your first reaction, if you looked at the book's patterns before now, could well have been, "But where's the body holding all those bits together?" Hopefully, now you can begin to see why the body isn't there. For a personalized fit, it's potentially easier, faster, and more accurate to drape the body pieces into shape than to start with the wrong shapes and to try to fix them.

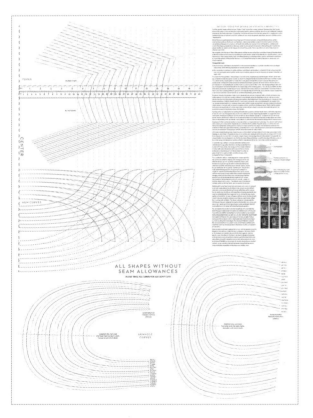

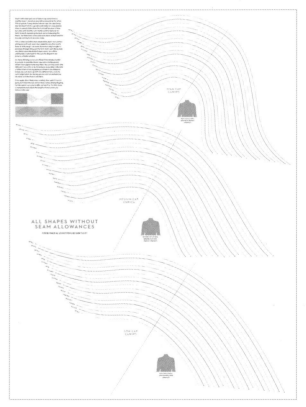

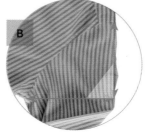

MEASURE A FAVORITE SHIRT

A good first step when choosing your best three starting pattern shapes is to measure those three shapes on at least one shirt you can wear comfortably in the shoulders and, particularly, in the armholes and sleeves. It doesn't matter if any other parts or details, like the neckline, body ease, hem or sleeve lengths, aren't right, or even how well this shirt seems to fit overall. You don't need to copy the yoke from the same shirt as for the sleeve and armhole lengths. We're just looking for ballpark starting dimensions for each of these three critical elements, you aren't committing to, or actually fitting anything at this stage, so there isn't a right or wrong selection at this point.

Lay the shirt out flat:

A Measure the yoke across the back about midway between the back/yoke seam and the neckline.

B Lay out one sleeve flat with the underarm seam at one edge. Measure across the sleeve width from the underarm/side seam (bottom of the armhole) to the opposite fold, keeping the measuring tape at 90 degrees to the fold. Pin-mark that spot on the fold, then measure the cap height from the pin mark, along the fold, up to the armhole seam.

C Measure both the front and back armhole seams by holding the measuring tape on edge. Add these two measurements to determine the total length. This measurement also represents the cap length.

You'll need these measurements at the start of the first how-to-drape chapter, on page 32. The sleeves and armholes raise several interesting points on using patterns when draping, so a brief discussion follows.

DRAPING WITH PATTERNS

A pattern for a shirt (or any garment) is a precise collection of flat, fixed-shape pieces with edges that fit together into garments with a known fixed shape. For this to work, each piece in the collection must be carefully matched to every other piece on all the edges.

When draping a shirt to fit, you'll eventually need the same collection of flat pieces as the pattern provides, but you don't start out with them. Instead, you begin with a single, not-yet-fixed yoke shape then cut front and back joining pieces and mold all these to the body. Only after this draping process do you discover the custom shape of the actual pattern pieces.

In other words, you don't yet know the finished shapes of the pattern pieces before you cut them from the test fabric, nor do you know the final shape the garment until you have finished and the shirt fits well. For this to work, you need to proceed in a fixed, logical order (yoke, body, armholes, sleeves), rough-cutting fabric pieces when you are ready to drape the next pattern piece (example: back of shirt to the yoke). This way, any seam or design line adjustments ripple through the process in the same order.

Happily, it is easy to combine both garment-making approaches—flat-pattern making and draping—to join the precision of a pattern to the flexibility of draping. This happens by choosing to precut from an existing pattern some pieces from the collection of needed parts, leaving the rest to be cut roughly for draping/shaping. You can also choose to precut only some edges on any piece, leaving the other edges rough cut for draping. And you can always remold even precision-cut fabric shapes as they appear on the form, in context, and in drape-to-fit order.

Here's an example: In the nutshell version of my process, (see page 15) I started with a yoke cut from a specific pattern. I also added a precise pair of armhole curves and a matching sleeve cap, all also traced from a specific pattern, so I'd have fabric versions of my three connected ovals from page 14.

My original plan was that the only thing I'd be draping with these precut shapes was the shape of the yoke holding them together. I wouldn't need to drape the sleeve and armhole shapes, just transfer the design lines for them, unchanged, from my pattern, regardless of how the yoke in between would be shaped, as shown.

This draping would be little more than a way to capture the shoulder slope of the form (or body), based on how the yoke molded to it.

But note that the only thing that allows me to actually capture the draped yoke's shape is the back and front pieces, which I didn't precut at all. I have to drape those two pieces before I even get to the armholes.

You'll recall that in the nutshell demonstration (see page 16) I did wind up changing the back armhole curves to correct the side-seam balance. To stick with my goal of not messing with the pattern-derived armholes or sleeve cap, I would just retrace or redraw each armhole curve, so together they'd regain the original overall length, but, in fact, I saw that a smaller armhole would probably work better. This is a good example of how draping often visually suggests new options worth considering as you progress. It also confirms how critical the order of progress is when draping, so you can be more flexible to making changes. I'd have been wiser to select my sleeve cap after I'd joined and balanced the side seams, and seen their impact on the armholes.

Here are a few more options for distributing the precut and rough-cut edges at the start of a shirt-draping process. In each diagram at right below, the black-outlined edges are the pattern curves I traced from a pattern with regular seam allowances and did not change; the red-outlined edges indicate those that I traced from a pattern but gave deep seam allowances, for maximum flexibility while draping. The gingham-like shapes are those I did not cut with edges from a pattern at all. Note

that it's perfectly okay to combine different methods in a single piece.

Let's go over the options in detail:

A It's ideal when you've got a pattern or copied garment you like a lot, and you just don't want to mess with sleeves and armholes, but still want to drape to correct for your shoulder slope, and you'd also maybe like to experiment with the ease and shaping of the side and underarm seams below the armholes.

B This option preserves side and/or underarm shaping from a favorite pattern, favorite shirt, or previous drape, precutting those seams, while leaving both the armholes and sleeve caps cut loose for further adjustments and experimentation. Note that I've given the yoke here black outlines, to indicate that I'd retain edge placement to preserve some interesting shaping from a pattern or other inspiration. This won't interfere with molding the yoke to conform to unique body contours; I just won't need to refold the ends or edges. Also note that the rough hem edge is required whenever there's uncertainty about where the front and back upper-body edges will wind up (and there almost always is uncertainty).

C This is my most common approach, the one in which I leave off any armhole or side-seam preshaping in favor of improvising when I get to them. I also cut the sleeve cap and underarm loose so they can be draped into shape.

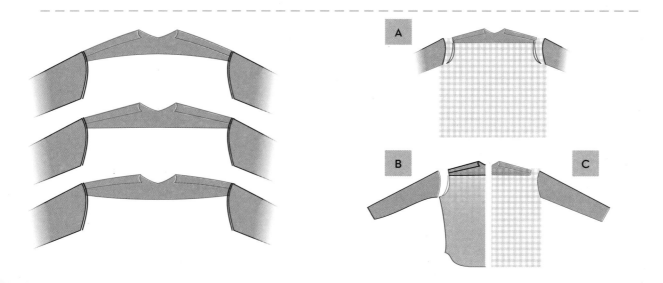

HOW TO USE ARMHOLE AND SLEEVE CAP CURVES

Being able to insert an already well-drafted, already-matched armhole and sleeve-cap shape (taken from a pattern) into a custom draped shirt with no changes needed is definitely a great thing, well worth taking advantage of, and perfect for beginners to the whole draping process. But because it is difficult to predict changes and further adjustments that might be made to the yoke and side seams as you adjust grain, balance, and fitting ease, it's very likely that a precut armhole will need to be eventually redrawn or retraced.

New armhole curves can be easily marked directly on the still-draped fronts and back, after the side and yoke seams are finalized. This is why my list of required starting shapes for draping has shrunk to include a collection of only yokes and a set of sleeve cap curves.

If you don't plan to start with an existing sleeve cap and armhole curve (from a pattern or traced from a shirt): mark an armhole on your drape, following the basic shape of the form. Once it appears to look like a well-shaped armhole, measure its total length, and check this against the measurement you took from your favorite shirt (see page 19). Adjust the shape of the curve, as needed to match the length measurements. Then, select the medium-height sleeve cap with the curve (from the multisize pattern provided or another source) that most closely matches the measurement. Trace the curve on to test fabric (with an inch (2.5 cm) or more of seam allowance at the cap) and stitch a sample sleeve with a softly tapered straight underarm seam, approximately 12" (30 cm) long. Pin the sample sleeve to the armhole, starting at the top—with the seam allowances pinned over the marked curve lines or fold the seam allowances to the wrong side and then pin the seamlines together.

With this very basic, and most typical, test sleeve, you'll be able to drape a lot of sleeve style variations. This is exactly what you'll see I've done throughout the following pages; I simply used the same red and white plaid sample sleeves over and over.

Here's the interesting part: These same sleeves also worked fine even if I had to adjust the width at the underarms to get them to baste nicely into the often quite different armhole curves. This confirms the two most basic truths I know regarding shirt sleeves:

1. Any sleeve cap shape can be fitted to any armhole as long the lengths of the seams (sleeve cap and armhole opening) match.

2. Any sleeve you specifically drape or adjust to look or feel good on you (or any fittee) is as good, if not better, than any predrafted one.

WORKING WITH CAP HEIGHT

The top three pairs of diagrams, below, illustrate one logic behind having a choice of sleeve-cap shapes such as I've provided on the book's pattern sheet: The taller the cap, the steeper the sleeve angle, and the narrower the sleeve tube, if all else is equal. The steeper the sleeve angle when worn, the less excess fabric there will be to bunch up at the underarm when the arms are down, and the more strain there will be on the garment when the arms are raised. Thus, working or sport shirts tend to have shallow caps and dressier shirts taller ones. So, you can choose any cap you want without changing the armhole you're comfortable with to get different sleeve angles. But only you can decide which you'll like best once you're wearing it.

However, there are factors other than sleeve angle to consider. The trio of diagrams, below, shows how the amount by which your armhole extends beyond your shoulder point is an equally useful determining factor for cap-height selection and has an equal impact on sleeve angle as well. The final illustration shows how a tall cap decreases in height if you make the sleeve tighter. Because the armhole is raised at the bottom to preserve the range of motion, bringing the sleeve's underarm seams up at the same time, reduces the cap height.

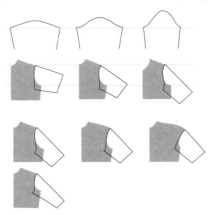

Fortunately, we're draping, not drafting our sleeves, so we can simply refine all these factors by adjusting the sample sleeve right on the form or body, finding the unique cap shape and height that will in fact work best regardless of whatever shape or curve is precut.

Ease around the arms at any point below the cap is controlled by shaping the underarm seam lines, which certainly don't have to be straight, and rarely are on modern shirts. The illustration shows a variety of interesting underarm curves, pulled from a collection of sleeve patterns.

But because it's very hard to find or make an accurate arm form, or to effectively evaluate any sleeve without actually trying it on and moving in it, fitting a sleeve is best done by pinning it onto the body drape and then slipping the test drape on to the actual body.

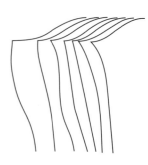

CAN I DRAPE PLUSSIZES AND WEIGHTLIFTERS, TOO?

One of the great features of this draping process is that it's completely shape neutral. It's about the ability to respond to the basic facts of gravity working on fabric when it is placed on a torso form or a body, any body—any shape. So, the main draping limitations you're likely to encounter are your own preconceptions about what looks good. And you can be sure that there's nothing about any particular body shape that would make draping a less intuitive or appropriate technique for fitting it. Just the opposite, I'd suggest!

The same goes for the body-wrapping technique I introduce on page 84. There's no method I know of that's as fast a path to either (or both) a highly detailed and accurate dress-form cover or an equally accurate basic body-shaped flat pattern, both of which I've found to be essential tools for working with unique body shapes.

The images, below, well demonstrate a few facts about bodies, fit, and fabric that all fitters will benefit from considering.

A This shows how an adult body can only grow or shrink in width, not height, unlike how most pattern-size grading operates, which is to always add or remove height. Hopefully, you can now begin to imagine how easily sleeve draping could capture the unique upper-arm curves on each body shown.

B These photos confirm that the more a closely a garment is fitted in one position, the more poorly it fits when we take another position.

B and **C** Different fabrics have different effects. Crisp fabrics better conceal body shapes than softer fabrics, but wrinkle more dramatically in response to body movement.

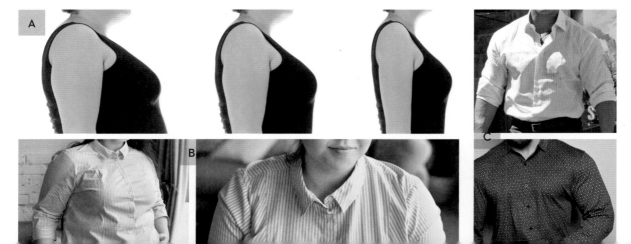

WRINKLE BASICS

There are two kinds of garment-fitting wrinkles, excess length wrinkles and strain wrinkles. The body, below, is too short for the blue shirt where the horizontal wrinkles appear, and it's too long for it where the vertical ones appear (so these wrinkles could just as well be called insufficient-length wrinkles). In this case, these conditions are probably temporary, simply caused by body movement, like most wrinkles in shirts. But also note that the body in the striped shirt is moving much more dramatically, yet relatively few wrinkles appear. This is simply because the fabric (possibly a knit) is stretched tight

on it. There's neither excess nor insufficient length to allow wrinkling in the sleeve, no matter how the wearer moves. But her reaching movement is temporarily reducing her body length in back, causing an excess length in the fabric and, thus, wrinkles just above her belt. By the way, notice how few wrinkles appear in the interesting vintage shirts she's hanging on the line, and imagine how easy it would be to more carefully pin each one to drape even more wrinkle-free from the line.

EXCESS LENGTH

STRAIN

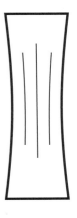

WRINKLE REMOVAL

Instead of pinning shirts to fall smoothly from a clothes line, consider the possibilities of pinning (draping) a single piece of fabric to a flat vertical surface, supporting it only from the top, as most simple garments are supported on bodies. In other words, let's look briefly at wrinkles in two-dimensions, without the 3D complexities of a body involved.

To arrange two-dimensional folds or wrinkles in some attractive, appealing way we have a lot of options, but little objective guidance, just our own opinions about what's attractive to direct our draping.

But there are two possible and obvious moves: Compress the outer top edges of the fabric in towards each other to create some specific amount of excess fabric to begin with, and then lift selected points along the top edge to divide and distribute the excess fabric.

Lifting just the right amount, and in the right location, may take some trial and error, but worthwhile to explore interesting ways to distribute the excess fabric.

To remove or reduce the folds we essentially have the same options: Stretch or smooth the upper edge so there's little or no excess length to fall into folds to begin with, then lift and pin the upper edge wherever it's drooping.

Removing folds or wrinkles is obviously easier than adding them. You see right way when the excess folds of fabric are gone, and whether you aligned the upper edge to be level, and if you put in enough well-positioned pins to keep any part of the upper edge from flopping over—no instructions needed, just paying attention and taking some care.

In short, no matter what draped or smoothed effects we explore, all we are doing is choosing points along the upper edge from which to let gravity arrange the fall of the fabric below. When choosing a smooth look, we have a clear limit (the width of the fabric) to work towards, while choosing to create drapey folds opens a host of possibilities.

You might be thinking that adding folds is like design, and removing them is like fitting, and I'd agree, while insisting that both adding and removing folds could as reasonably be considered both fitting or design. Either way, removing folds/wrinkles is the essence of the basic draping we'll be doing with the main, large, rectangular pieces of fabric (fronts, backs) as we fit, that is: Smooth and Lift—it's that simple. We'll have real body shapes underneath to make the process seem more complex and the range of possible wrinkles more challenging, but our possible moves will remain the same. Smooth and lift.

When we add another large fabric piece to the project and attempt to join it to the first (like the shirt back to the shirt front or vice versa), in either two- or three-dimensions, we introduce the issue of how to join two pieces without spoiling the smooth, wrinkle-free drape of the first piece. We must first bring them together, or cut their joining edges, so there's sufficient length to begin with, then smooth and lift one or both pieces in relation to the other so there's no strain or ill-placed lifting introduced on either side. So, with more fabric pieces there are more edges to handle, but our possible moves remain pretty much the same—smooth and lift. Now we just have to balance these moves between multiple pieces: Smooth and lift, then balance. Repeat.

The bottom line: Whenever you're draping to fit, and maybe feel stuck, just ask: "Where can I smooth, lift, or balance here?" And as you view all the draping demonstrations that follow, that's basically all you'll see me doing.

PIN- AND WHEEL-TRACING

An essential fitting and pattern-making skill is the accurate transfer of marked, seamed, or cut fabric onto paper to create patterns. Wheel-tracing is how I transfer markings from draped fabric, like the marked lines on the blue gingham shown here. Pin-tracing, as shown on the yellow plaid shirt, is my process for transferring pattern shapes from existing garments onto paper.

In either case, I depend on large sheets of plain paper and an equally large soft, pinnable surface, because each process involves fabric laid smooth over the paper and the seams or markings traced by poking pins or wheel-teeth through all the layers into something soft underneath them all. A roll of pattern tissue and an ironing board serves well for small shapes, but for full-garment pattern-making my main supplies are a pad of plain flip-chart paper (easily stored with no curling from being rolled) and a sheet or two of foam core sufficient to fit under the full size of the top paper. For pin-tracing, I like to hold a heavy sewing-machine needle in a pin vise; and any sort of toothed tracing wheel will work for wheel tracing.

It's easy to trace the yoke, sleeve cap, and armholes from an existing shirt for future draping into a custom pattern—and please note, once again, that these are the only parts of any shirt or pattern you need for this. The critical thing in every case is to confirm that the grain is straight and square on each garment part being traced before you begin. Plaid fabrics are obviously helpful for this, as are gridded quilting reference rulers, as are used in the sleeve and armhole photos at lower right.

To capture the full yoke width and shape (**A**) and the sleeve cap shape (**B**), align the folded centers of these pieces with a centered fold of a piece of paper as shown; pin to secure the layers, then trace exactly along all the seam lines by poking the pin or needle through the paper below.

Note the nonsymmetrical curves (between the front of the shirt and the back) often found on full sleeve cap seams (**B**); to accurately trace them, you need to feel through the layers to locate the hidden one, and pin trace that seam too. Each paper unfolds to reveal the full pattern, of course. You'll need a front and back armhole, so label these carefully (**C**), and it's a good idea to include a reference vertical grain line near each curve for easy alignment with centerfronts and centerback when transferring these to the draped front and back rectangles. But note: This amount of precision precut shaping is rarely needed or preserved when draping; it's replaced with customized curves revealed when the draped test sleeve is transferred to paper.

To capture a full pattern from an existing shirt, see the links to my website at dirtk.

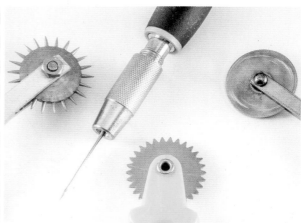

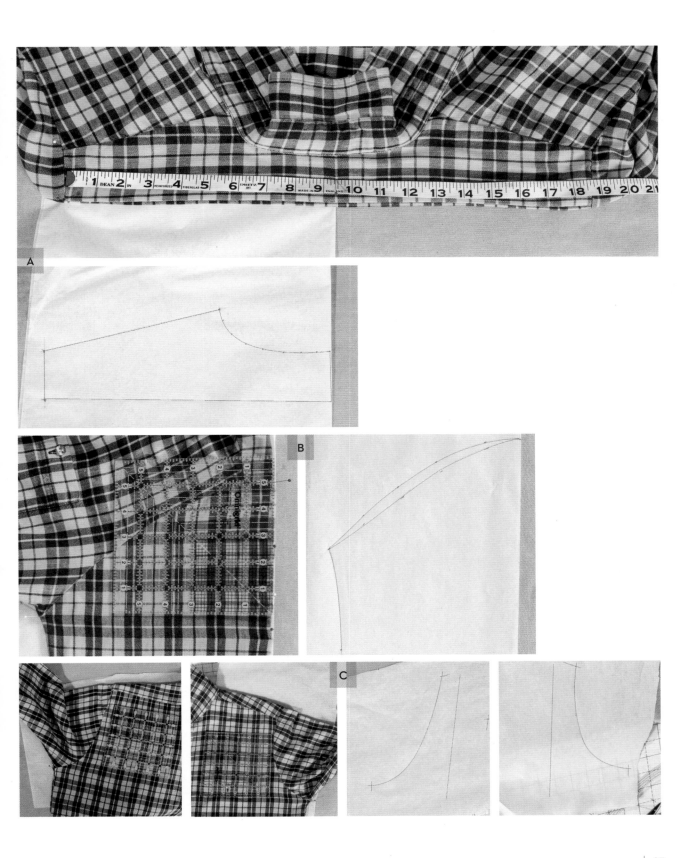

MEET THE FORM FAMILY

Initially, I hoped this book would feature lots of real-world bodies photographed in varying stages of draped projects, but it's even more difficult to find fitting process-shot volunteers than it is for custom clothiers to find customers who like long fitting sessions. I required, not just willing fit-volunteers, but volunteers with classic fitting issues and body asymmetry. Eventually, I accepted the reality that the best way to study fitting—especially fitting by draping—is to have your own customized dress form. Fitting buddies are great, but are usually nowhere to be found at 1 AM!

In lieu of willing fit volunteers, I created four torso forms, each one heavily customized so, together, they display as wide and as likely an assortment of common shoulder and other postural variations as I found possible. Two are based on real bodies and two are fictional bodies with plausible fit problems (based on much people watching, especially via the television; bless that pause button).

I've detailed just how I built each form at my blog—each quite different—and describe in some detail exactly how you can leverage part of my tight-fitting shirt process into a dress-form project as well (see page 86). Please ignore any seams or pinned tapes that are visible on the forms themselves. These are *not* guidelines for draping, as they might be on commercial forms. They're just random artifacts of making them easier to use.

The forms I use throughout the book are shown here, each with a short list of distinguishing shapes and characteristics. But as you'll learn, the drape-to-fit process doesn't require any such preliminary assessment because the process is not problem or shape specific. It simply responds, with equal effectiveness, to bodies of any size or shape.

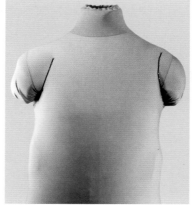 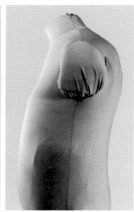

#1, REAL MALE BODY (ME)

- Slouched posture
- Rounded, protruding upper back
- Sloped, uneven shoulders
- Forward hips
- Same circumference from hips up

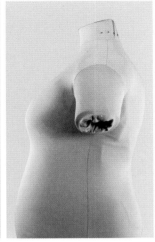
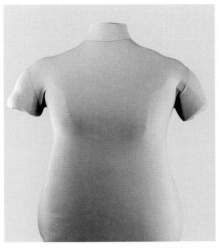

#2, REAL FEMALE BODY

- Plus-size
- Straight posture
- Somewhat rounded, protruding upper back
- Not very sloped, even shoulders
- Full, protruding chest
- Largest circumference at hips

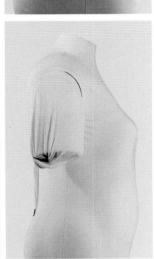

#3, FICTIONAL FEMALE BODY

- Erect posture
- Flat upper back
- Somewhat sloped, rounded, even shoulders
- Full, protruding chest
- About the same circumference from hips up

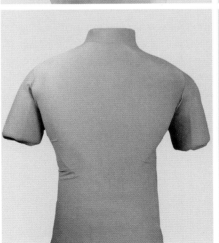
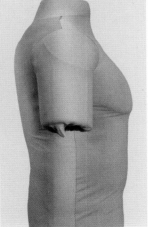

#4, FICTIONAL MALE BODY

- Athletic body
- Erect posture
- Very wide flat back
- Sloped, wide, deep, even shoulders
- Gradually protruding chest
- Less waist circumference than at chest

DRAPING ESSENTIALS YOU NEED TO KNOW

FABRIC-SMOOTHING REALITIES

While fitting loose garments traditionally is much less of a challenge than fitting tight ones, it's easier to drape tightly than loosely, and easier to remove ease than to add it. This is another way of saying that smoothing away wrinkles is easier than creating them in the first place.

It's generally true that diagonal or horizontal garment wrinkles are almost always indicators of poor fit, while vertical wrinkles, especially at the sides, can often be attractive, as well as helpful for easy arm movement; this sort of visible ease is in fact often called "drape." But to create drape like this is not as easy to do when draping to create a snug, smooth fit. I'll address this in the demonstrations to follow.

Similarly, convex shapes are easier to drape (and fit) than concave ones, so bodies with few concavities are generally easier to drape. You can allow enough extra length for the fabric to fall into a concave space, but how do you keep it there if gravity isn't helping (as it definitely does on yokes, for example, which are more or less held in place by the weight of the body and sleeve fabrics)? Stretching fabric over and across concavities, which might occur between the center front and a forward shoulder on a stooped figure (one of my own issues), is an option to explore if the garment fabric is soft and heavy.

ASYMMETRY

Draping, by nature, is great at capturing unique body shapes, so it has no problem with asymmetry. In fact, it has more trouble with symmetry! It's up to the draper to ensure symmetry, because draping on its own won't; it will automatically capture asymmetry if it's there, and if it isn't, it's still hard to ensure you're draping perfectly identical sides. This is why draping for commercial, noncustom work is typically done on only half the form. The draped results are simply mirrored to create a full garment or pattern, which can be cut on a fabric fold or double layer. Custom fit, particularly when there are asymmetric issues, requires a full-body drape.

While almost all bodies are somewhat asymmetrical, many can be fitted perfectly well with symmetrical garments, which are a lot faster to cut than asymmetrical ones. So, it's up to you to decide whether it's worth your time and effort to correct the fit of asymmetrical pattern pieces from a full garment drape or to test the full drape and then decide which side fits best and simply mirror that side. This may well be different, depending on the garment and/or the fabric you are draping, since looser garments are more forgiving about matching the body exactly than tighter ones.

For the same reasons, draping isn't easy to do exactly the same way more than once, so you'll likely notice that a re-drape on the same body with the same starting shapes and the same test fabrics could easily turn out slightly differently each time, but in each case, fit just as well.

THE FABRIC REALLY MATTERS! AND YOU'LL NEED PLENTY . . .

Depending as it does so thoroughly on the flexibility of fabric, draping is most definitely a process for which different fabrics can make a huge difference in your results, to the extent, for example, of eliminating or requiring darts that other fabrics did or didn't require. As you'll see in the project chapters, I've often re-draped a previously draped basic muslin in a fabric more like one I want to use for a specific planned garment, just to be sure the same adjustments will work in the fashion fabric. I also, now that I know better, simply cut out the fashion fabric for each new shirt project with plenty of draping allowance, ensuring that I've got wiggle room when the drapability of the fashion fabric doesn't fully replicate the draping fabric; keeping in mind that initial basic draping results for any particular project, even if very close, are typically still approximate starting points.

Clearly, all this draping means you're going to have to increase your available stash of test fabrics! You'll have noticed my preference for woven (as opposed to printed) plaids and ginghams, because their contrasting, crossing yarns provide essential grain information. I use unwashed lightweight, polyester-blend ginghams as my default crisp-fabric, drape-to-fit, full-body "muslins," and usually only use traditional beige or solid-color muslin fabrics for smaller detail and design experiments for which grain is just as critical but doesn't need to be as constantly visible or potentially distracting. I collect these fabrics in various weights and crispness and I don't prewash any of them. Lightweight cotton flannel plaids are excellent for soft-fabric draping, and plaid or checked medium-weight woolens are great for outerwear draping. And I regularly re-sort my main fabric stash to further separate the test fabrics from the garment fabrics; it's a great way to feel better about all those impulse buys that have lost their allure.

CONVERTING DRAPES TO PATTERNS

Assuming your goal is to have a precise paper pattern when you're done, draping is, of course, only the start of the process. You'll next need to use something like the tracing tools described in "Pin- and Wheel-Tracing," page 26, to transfer and record the marked seamlines from your test-fabric drape onto paper. These tracings will then need further refinement to become patterns you can cut use, truing all the lines to match where they join and blending them smoothly where they cross. This is a very well-documented process, so I'll refer you to the Resources on page 140 for more information along with the online material.

What I didn't expect before I started experimenting with draping-to-fit, is how much it would change the way I use paper shirt patterns altogether. I now cut all fashion fabrics with generous draping allowances at all side, armhole, and shoulder seams, knowing that I'll find the exact stitching lines for these seams, not from the pattern, but by draping them afresh for each new project and in the chosen fabric. You'll find specific examples of exactly how I do this in the project chapters, and you'll find that it can vary considerably, depending on the details and fabrics involved. In general, my every shirt project now starts with a drape, to establish how much ease I want for the basic silhouette, around which I then arrange seamlines and allowances for whatever details I want to add, some of which, such as hems, can only be generously approximated. So, for me, draping is no longer simply a fitting and pattern-making first step. It's become an integral part of the construction process, allowing me to better respond to individual fabrics and unique details as I craft them together, not constrained by precisely precut pieces.

QUICK OR SLOW?

Personally, this drape-to-fit process fits my tendency to work slowly and cautiously, being more concerned with flexibility than efficiency; in fact, I admit it has actually slowed me down, with a clear benefit to my results. Plus, as I worked through all the examples shown in this book, I've definitely erred on the side of multiple repeat test drapes, for the sake of my own doubled certainty. But rest assured, draping to fit can just as easily offer a very quick path to truly customized patterns especially if you don't want or plan to re-drape every time. The choice is yours, and there are plenty of options between the two extremes.

FIT | 3
DRAPING THE LOOSE-FITTING SHIRT
WHAT ARE LOOSE-FITTING SHIRTS?

In this chapter, we explore how to use the drape-to-fit process to create custom-fitted shirt patterns for shirts with the following features:

- Straight side seams

- No darts

- Both fitted and dropped shoulders

- Maximized freedom of movement in the arms and shoulders

- Enough body ease to drape without wrinkles and without matching or revealing the shape of the body within

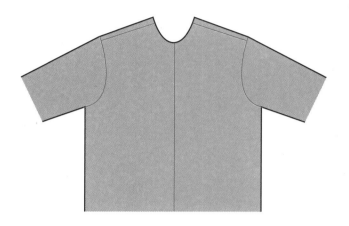

Fitted loose shirts are those that fit only with any precision through the shoulders and are, thus, for our purposes, custom-shaped to the wearer only there. Note in the diagram at right that there are no darts and only the basic seams of a typical shirt. While this is generally the most basic and easiest shirt style to drape, it introduces almost all the draping-to-fit issues we'll encounter in this learning process, and will challenge us to deal right up front with loose draping, which is often a bit more demanding than adjusting fabric to fit snugly. Snug fitting always pushes right up against the solid boundary of the form being draped, while loose draping always involves at least a few arbitrary judgements about where and how far exactly to position the fabric away from the form, as well as, questions on how to control the fall of fabric that isn't touching the body or form.

Since this chapter is our overall introduction to the draping process, we'll proceed slowly to discover the many options that can apply to all styles, but may not be addressed as thoroughly in subsequent chapters, so please read through this chapter even if loose fit isn't your preferred style option. But, rest assured that there's no definitive line between loose and fitted shirts, nor any reason not to add some shaping or tapering to the side seams when accommodating a loose drape. Go ahead and shape the shirt anyway you like! Once you have the perfectly draped muslin, the test muslin you want to use to create the paper pattern, download the pdf, "Converting a muslin drape to a paper pattern" at www.quartoknows.com/page/sewing-shirts.

Also, recall from the discussion on page 20 that draping to fit only the shoulders is perfectly appropriate when copying a shirt with shaping you like everywhere except the shoulders. In this case, drape to improve the shoulder fit to match your shoulder slope or possible asymmetry, and preserve the fit elsewhere, including any existing side-seam shaping.

HOW TO CHOOSE YOUR YOKE

Since all our draping projects, for every level of fitting ease, begin with a draped-to-fit yoke, I'll cover that process in detail, demonstrating on each of the four fitting forms. And, I'll use the multisize yoke pattern included in this book.

Measure either the existing yoke of a comfortable or favorite shirt or the body itself. Don't fret over either measurement, since you'll be customizing the actual ends of the yoke once it is on the body/form. To the measurements, add at least an inch (2.5 cm) of extrawide seam allowances, or even more if you're not sure about what you'll eventually feel most comfortable wearing.

To measure a yoke on a shirt, measure a little above the back/yoke seam.

To measure a body, hold a tape measure straight across the back between shoulder points that look like good yoke-end points to you.

1 Near the edge of a piece of tracing paper, lay out a horizontal line equal to half your measured yoke length, then align this line with the pattern's ruler so the beginning edge of the ruler is in position at what represents the center back of the yoke, and tape it down removably. At the end of the horizontal line (opposite from the center back), draw a vertical line long enough to cross one of the yoke outlines above.

2 Trace around the yoke outline that intersects with the line you just drew, roughing in a neckline as shown, to be later refined on the form.

3 Add plenty of extra play-around seam allowance width at the neck line and ends. Square out the seam allowances, as shown. Add regular width seam allowances to the straight edges at the shoulder and bottom edges. This is your yoke pattern.

4 Fold your test fabric in half on the cross grain. Position the center back of the pattern on the fabric fold. Cut out a single layer fabric yoke on the lengthwise grain. Maintain the extrawide seam allowances; and we will determine how much to fold or trim by draping this oversize shape on the torso form (or the body).

Tip: I prefer to use fairly heavyweight test fabric for the yoke, usually not the same fabric I use to drape the front, back and sleeve, because the finished yoke of a shirt is a double layer, so a heavier fabric better simulates a real yoke.

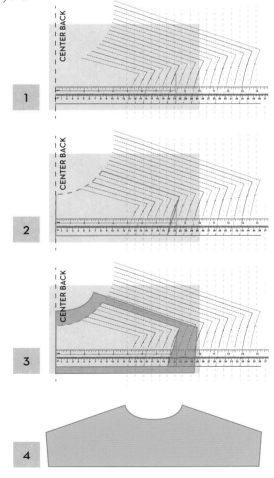

POSITIONING THE YOKE

Once you have cut out your yoke, you can start draping. On the following pages, I'll demonstrate how to position an identically rough-cut yoke on all four of our different shaped forms so you can start to see how the results vary, depending more upon unique body shapes than on the original cut yoke shape.

Note that everything I'm doing on a form can be as easily done on a live body. Just have the fittee wear their usual upper-body under garments, if any, and have a tight-fitting T-shirt or turtleneck on, so you can pin things to them securely and comfortably. Also note that in all these photos that I'm simply making visual judgements about what to do, measuring nothing except by eye.

In each case, I start by centering the shaped (back) neck-line on the form neck, positioning it as far up as it will easily go, and pin it there. Then I evaluate, from all four sides, how the yoke appears everywhere else. Since the seam allowances are wider than usual, you'll probably need to make multiple clips into them at the neckline to allow the yoke to sit more smoothly around the neck and more forward over the shoulders. Don't hesitate to cautiously cut away extra fabric because if you take away too much you can always indicate where to add it back when you trace off the draped yoke.

On Form #1 just a few short clips into the neck seam allowance allow the yoke to fall closer to the neck and to move forward on the shoulders. Overall, I am pleased with the width of the yoke, so there is no need to fold the ends under to make the yoke narrower, since this rounded upper back requires extra fabric.

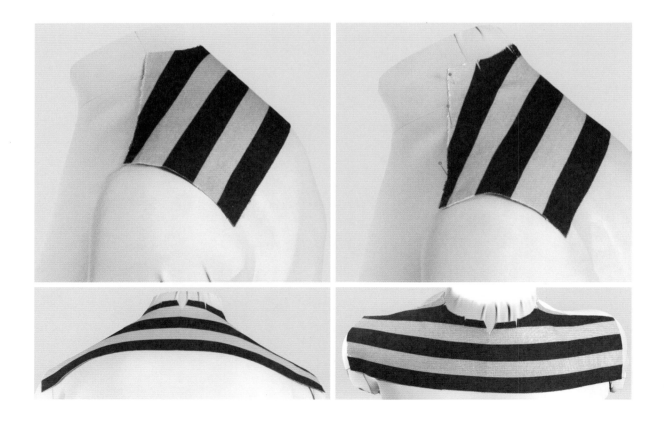

On Form #2, once again, a few clips into the neckline seam allowance works wonders to settle the yoke onto the shoulders. Because the back-edge of the yoke is much wider than it needs to be (**A**, **B**), I folded under the yoke ends at each shoulder to reduce the width (**B**, **C**). The right yoke front edge extends further forward (**D**) compared to the left one, so I folded that edge under to make them more symmetric (**E**).

On Form #3, as usual, I've once again improved the lay of the yoke and shifted it slightly forward by clipping into the neckline seam allowance. But in this case, we're seeing something new: The bottom (back) yoke edge extends beyond the curve of the back, so it sticks up above and away from the body on each side (**A**, **B**). The solution is simple, I folded up the whole bottom edge, as I folded under the yoke ends, bringing the bottom edge back into contact with body (**C**).

Also note how the yoke width in front, which I reduced by folding under the ends and is exposing quite a bit of the upper arm, is still considerably wider than the width of the body at the armpits (**D**). I'm guessing that this will allow enough width in front to cover the bust; if not, I'll let the yoke unfold in front for more width (later in the draping process).

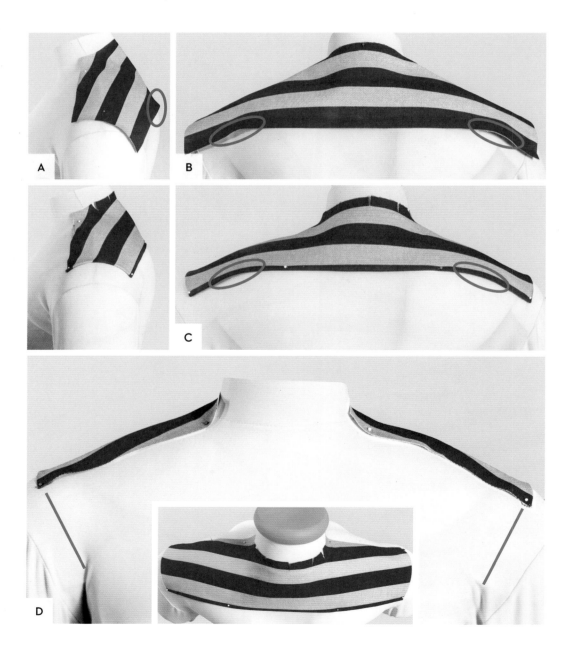

On Form #4, nothing about the yoke placement is new, including my decision to fold the ends under quite a bit, exposing a lot of upper arm beyond the ends. My decision is based on how wide the source shirt (from which I took the initial yoke measurement to cut yokes for all four forms) appeared to be in back when I tried it on this form. I'll see how it works out when I drape the back.

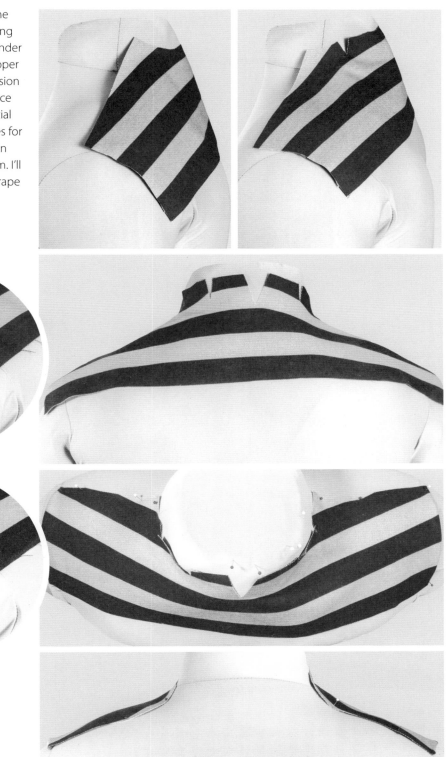

RESHAPING THE YOKE

By far, the most common practice in manufactured shirts is for minimal or no shaping on any of the seam edges where the yokes join to body pieces; they're all straight lines as in the diagram at top right. And if there is any shaping, it's commonly applied only to the front- and back-to-yoke edges, so the yoke itself remains straightedged, no matter how much it may have curve to adapt to the body shapes inside.

This logic is perfect for my drape-to-fit process since the yoke can be cut simply and molded to the body. The fronts and backs are more precisely (and usually asymmetrically) draped, and then cut, to match the molded yoke shapes, with no need to recut the yoke. As you can see in the bottom diagram of the shaped yoke, this also makes good visual sense if a stripe or plaid is involved, because it keeps the yoke-to-back edge parallel to both the seamline and the stripes. Asymmetrically shaped pattern pieces are usually less distracting when at least one piece has stripes parallel to the seam between them.

Curving one seam edge that will join to a straight edge effectively causes the seam to act like a dart, so it's been my practice, when fitting yokes and backs to any nonflat upper back, to first alter the yoke length so it crosses the apex or most curved part of the shoulder curves in the same way that a front princess seam crosses the bust point.

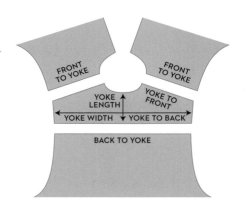

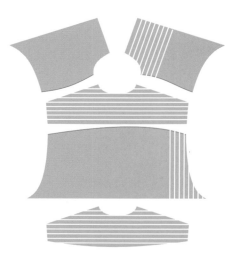

FINDING THE APEX OF SHOULDER CURVES

One easy way to find the apex of curved shoulders is to drape a piece of fabric over the back and across the shoulders to see if and where it naturally forms the appearance of one or more darts as the orange gingham does in the top two images on page 39. If you'd like to replace these darts completely with shaping at each end of the back-to-yoke seam, you'll need to recut the yoke so it is long enough that it reaches down to the dart points of the fold on the draped back. This allows the yoke-to-back edge to conform naturally to the body, and shows you when draping the back to the yoke, exactly how to cut the back-to-yoke edge to match the shape and length of the molded yoke edge.

But you'll probably notice in these photographs that the dart on the right is slightly shorter than the dart on the left (**A**). In many instances, lengthening the yoke to the dart-end area still allows the yoke mold itself to reflect the asymmetrical roundness of the shoulders and thus minimize the dart differences. An easier and more flexible solution would be to simply make tucks or gathers out of the dart excess as shown below, eliminating any need to recut the yoke.

Simply folding over the excess dart fabric to create tucks, around where the darts appeared (**B**, **C**), is an easier solution than reshaping the back-to-yoke seam. Tucks are more flexible than seams, and the seam itself will be less radically curved if it's not absorbing all the reshaping, so it will more respond better to shoulder movement.

Gathers, pleats, and tucks are design-flexible because of the different ways they can be converted, redistributed, and expanded. Note how the box pleat (**D**) is providing additional ease because it's not unfolding below the curve to absorb the dart excess as it is in the example on the bottom right (**E**).

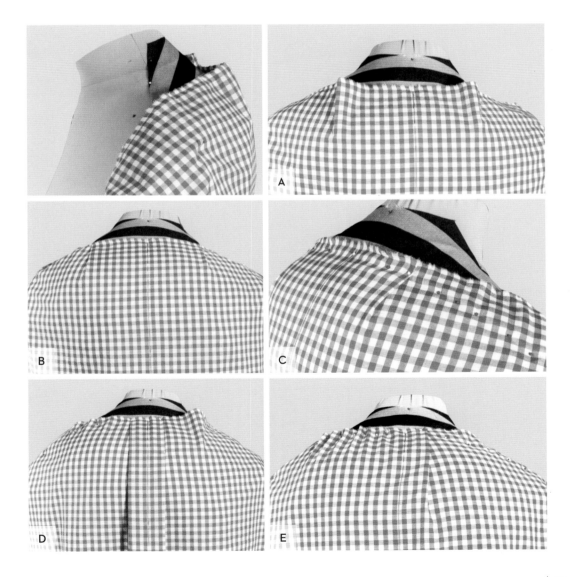

DRAPING FITTED SHOULDERS

After molding the yoke, the first step is to determine the size of the front and back draping rectangles. A quick eye-measure of half the form's circumference provides the minimum width for the draping rectangle; I add a good few inches (5 cm) to each side. The length should at least just enough to reach the hips from the center-back neck. Cut the draping rectangle for the front a few inches (5 cm) longer than the back rectangle so it reaches above the neckline to completely cover the yoke fronts.

Tip: Ginghams and plaids are the ideal for draping the front and back pieces—they make it so easy to see both grains.

PLACING THE RECTANGLES

I mark the centers of the draping rectangles and the yoke edges with a fabric marking pen or a small snip into the seam allowance. Then, once you are ready to place the rectangles, you can align the center markings.

Pin the back rectangle to the back yoke, first. Adjust the sides and top edges of the back rectangle until the woven plaid looks grain-square across the back over the shoulders. A few judicious clips into, but well short of, the likely armhole allows the sides to be pinned, too.

In front, you can estimate a small neckline curve at the top center, as I did in the nutshell demo, or simply slash a few inches (5 cm) down so the rectangle can slide easily around the neck and over the yoke. I use a plum line to adjust the vertical grain of the front rectangle to the form. Carefully lift and smooth each upper corner to straighten the crosswise grain, and then pin these into the yoke to secure them in place. I clipped into the armholes just as I did for the back rectangle. Finally, with cautious clipping and pinning, I can mold and position the upper edges of the rectangle around the neck and against the yoke's front edges in preparation for marking the seam lines there.

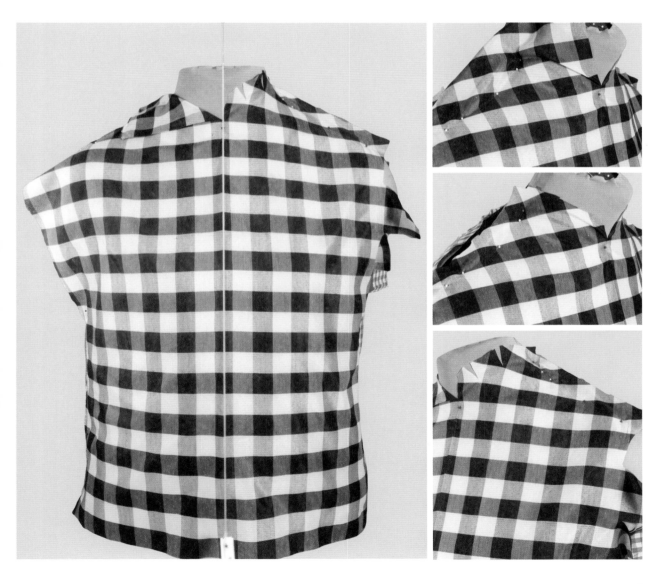

ADJUSTING THE SIDE SEAMS

Here's where the draping process really shines by clarifying and enabling subtle adjustments with a precision that would be impossible to guestimate using flat-pattern methods. Pinning the sides so the grains are parallel, I can see slight strain wrinkles coming down diagonally from the midback to the low side. Releasing the pins in the bottom half of the side seam lets the fronts and back separately relax to smoother positions, so I can easily re-pin them for a better hanging back and front rectangle.

I can't resist pinning away some of the excess fabric in the back, noting how much excess fabric I can pin out without shifting the pinned sides or adding strain wrinkles (more than 5 inches (12.5 cm) all together, at the hem). I also noted that the right side of the back needed less dramatic repinning to release fewer strain lines, once the grains were aligned, and that side, too, still looked fine after the back reduction. This is the beauty of draping, these kind of fitting adjustments, seem to happen automatically and precisely, clarifying and simplifying management of otherwise hard to see, and even harder to redraw or draft, asymmetries. Note that, so far, I've simply overlapped the front edges on the back ones and made no attempt to establish specific side-seam lines.

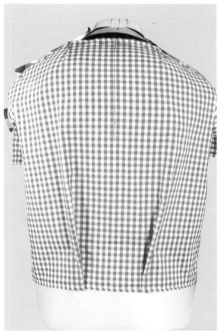

MARKING THE SEAMS

At this point, it is time to check the drape all around and mark along all the overlaps to create seam lines. I could have been marking these as I went, but in this case, I've waited until now when I can see the whole drape and possibly make further adjustments. To mark the side seams, slip a plastic ruler under the draped shirt so you can mark both layers at once. I place these seams visually, but you can certainly measure now, instead of later, to be more precise. The ruler will protect the form, or frittee, in case your marker bleeds through the fabric.

Along the folded-under yoke edges, I'd regularly pinned the rectangles to hold everything in place, which also simplifies accurate marking; simply use a marker to mark along the pins. At the ends, I mark both the rectangles and the yoke where I expect the armholes to begin.

To mark a first-draft neckline, I position a paper strip, about an inch (2.5 cm) wide over the neck and adjust it to establish, and then mark, a neckline around the bottom edge of the strip. All these markings are just first-draft beginnings, to be tested with machine basting and, probably, an additional test muslin.

Finally, I measure the shirt front, from side seam to side seam, and in various locations across the body so I can be very sure of positioning the side seams symmetrically when I true the traced pattern. I make note of the measurements to see if there's any dramatic nonsymmetry that I should both confirm and possibly leave in place to preserve the fitting information I already established.

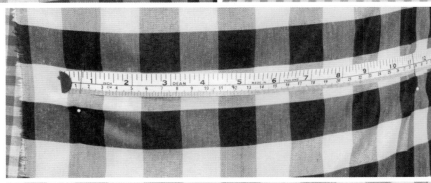

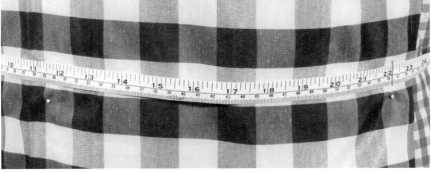

BASTED TEST

After marking the shoulder seam lines, it's time to baste the pieces together at the yoke. I start by machine basting the yoke seams to the front and back drapes. Once basted, it's time to examine the drape back on the form. I pin the side seams, as marked, and then I'm able to finagle the side seams back to being grainmatched and closerfitting without creating any strain lines, in part, because I'm shifting the seam lines inward here more than before, and perhaps because I also take the time to explore microshifting the sides up and down against one another, as detailed at right.

I'm not as interested in figuring why this worked so well, as I am in seeing how good everything is looking and how intuitive and tactile the process of getting here was. No doubt, I could have gotten to this point at the pre-basting stage, but I always seem to find I can do better on a second pass, which is why I make sure there are plenty of opportunities to redrape like this.

ARMHOLES

To shape and mark the armholes, I traced the front and back curves, without seam allowances, from the same source shirt where I got the yoke (see Pin-Tracing, page 26), onto printer paper. I trimmed these curves, as you can see at right, so I could manipulate them directly on the form with no stretching, but with the same bendability that will be required of the fabric, as shown below.

This form's right shoulder is quite a bit lower and rolls forward very differently compared to the left shoulder. This raises and enlarges the right front curve so it can't reach the back curve, causing both curves to pivot away from the yoke end and toward the side seam. With no arm in the way, it's easy to blend and mark a new armhole line between the curves, right on the fabric and still on the form.

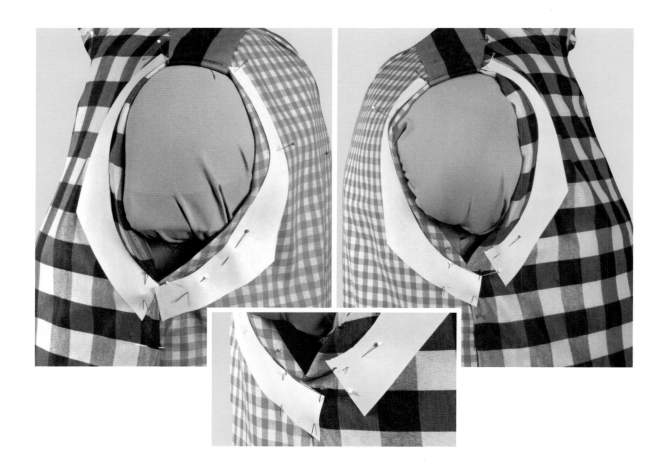

If you were fitting this on a body, you would need to assess the armhole curves with as little armraising as possible. It is much easier to do this flat on the muslin pieces after marking the final side seams and their alignment. And then, transfer the traced paper armhole curves with the test drape (muslin) flat on a table, with open side seams. Be sure to try the muslin back on and pin the side seams to check the alignment.

As another option, instead of using armhole curves from a source shirt, you can use armhole curves taken from the included pattern sheet. Choose a pair that matches the cap-length measurement from your source shirt as described on page 19, or measure the form or body once you have draped to this point. These curves meet at the shoulder top, making no allowance for a yoke, so they can be used with any yoke you wind up choosing and draping, unaffected by any draped yoke asymmetries, and easier to match to nonsymmetrical shoulders. No adjustment is needed, in this case, for the armhole curves to meet at the sides.

To use these curves, tentatively mark the shapes of the curves directly on the fabric. You'll measure the marked curves to determine armhole lengths. Do this enough and you'll soon find your premarked curves are much the same as those you traced for transferring from this or any other pattern source, so you can skip the transfer step and start trusting the curves you draw.

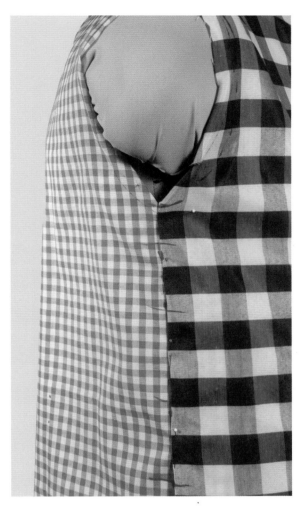

SLEEVE PIN-TEST

Here's the front view of the drape at this stage, with sample sleeves, pinned into the armhole openings.

For this step, you need to cut a pair of sleeves from any source that has a cap length that matches your armhole length. In this case, I traced one from the included pattern sheet with the medium-high cap (page 22).

Pin or machine baste the underarm seam. Starting at the top, pin the sleeve to the armhole aligning the cap with the armhole so it falls smoothly. As you can see, it's easy at this stage to slightly rotate the whole sleeve to position the grain, as needed, so it looks good and the fabric pattern is straight. If you're working on a form, though, be sure to test this on the real-life wearer, who may have

a different opinion based on comfort. Before you commit, you might find that matching the actual arm angle at rest works better than being theoretical about grain level. In the same vein, pay attention as you position and drape the sleeve, to the relationship between what the drape looks like and how it feels to the wearer when he or she is moving. Take time for multiple pinned or basted try-ons if you're working on a form and not directly on the wearer. Soon you'll develop a good sense of how the results from working on whatever form you've got are different from on-the-body results, and you'll see how you need to adjust the form or you will simply make mental notes of how to improve the drape for your wearer (see my blog for more on form adjusting).

BACK VIEW AND SHOULDER EASE

Here's the back view of the drape, at the same stage as the front view (see page 50), with sleeves pinned in place.

These other photos depict several views of the back armholes with a pinned sleeve, focusing on how much ease (for comfortable movement) there appears to be in the various shots and how much can be simulated.

In addition to the arm-angle/sleeve-rotation issue depicted on the front view, the impact a real arm and shoulder joint has on a drape at both the side seams and armholes can only be approximated on a form, because this will, of course, vary a lot in real wear, as the arm

moves against and away from the sides of the body in all sorts of different ways.

Sleeve position can only be truly evaluated with the test garment on the wearer, and judged by the wearer based on his or her own comfort requirements. On the form, however, you can at least pin or push the sides and the armhole curves in towards the body if they're not already fitted to be there. This simulates the impact of arms held still and close to the body, and it is reflected in the second of each of the photo pairs at the right.

We'll look next at a few ways to increase the ease at the armholes by draping loose shoulders.

DRAPING LOOSE SHOULDERS

You'll recall from the description (see page 32, start of this chapter) of the loose-fitting shirt that the shoulders and armholes of the draped test garment are all that need to match the body inside. For this next section, I am using my one homemade dress form with flexible arms.

In the previous pages ("Draping Fitted Shoulders," pages 40–41), we very carefully adjusted the fronts and backs as they met at the side seams to ensure that the shirt fell as smooth and straight as possible, while making no efforts to add further shaping to the shirt to reflect or match the body within. We'll explore those options in the next chapter. Even so, the shirt's shoulders and armhole positions were matched exactly to the body, because that's what draping does most naturally. If, instead, you want more ease in the shoulders and armholes, you'll need additional steps to loosen the shoulders of the drape.

MUSLIN 1: INITIAL DRAPE

My preferred method is to start with a loose drape adjust—demonstrated to create fitted shoulders and armholes—then alter the resulting pattern to extend them.

Note that for a loose drape on this particular form, I've tucked and lifted the back across the armholes to bring the side seams together smoothly and squarely, taking a bit more depth on the right side, as needed, for a smooth result on each side (**A**, **B**). I took care to angle the tuck smoothly across the full back so the pinned fabric would lay flat for pattern markings transfer once off the form. To trace the front and back armhole curves, I pivoted them from the respective yoke ends to the draped side seams, as shown at bottom far, right.

A

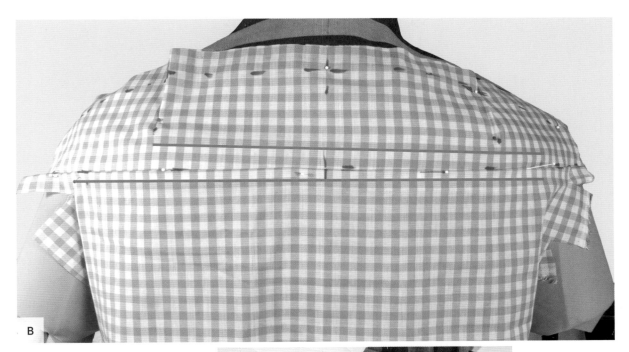

B

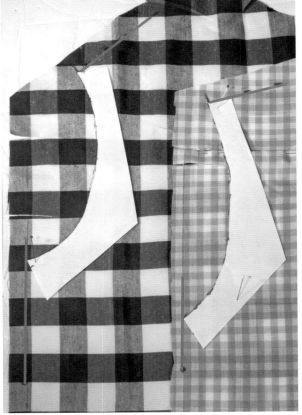

MUSLIN 2:
PROOF AND ARMHOLE SHIFT

The next step, shown here in plaid images, is not additional for me anyway; it's what I do after any initial drape. I make a basic (no details) proof muslin carefully stitched following an accurate tracing of the pieces from the first drape, minimally smoothed and/or straightened with rulers and curves. There's no point in proceeding without being sure the draped seam lines are good so far and possibly improvable. As expected, the fit across the shoulders and at the armholes is close, not loose, with very little further adjustment having been needed at or below the armholes, and none at the shoulders—which was our initial goal. So, now that I'm satisfied, I can proceed to drape loose shoulders by altering the pieces from the original drape.

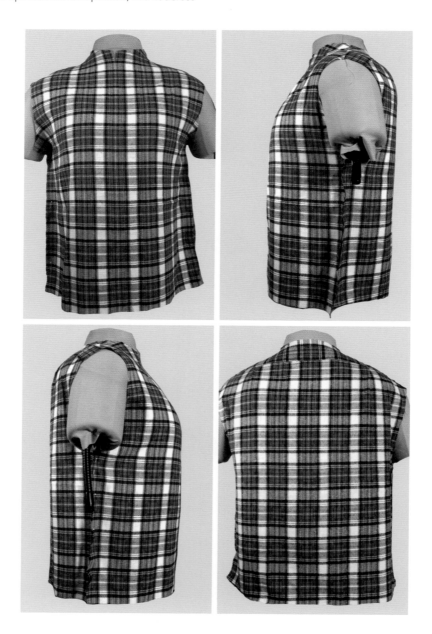

Now for the additional step shown below, at right. Although the proof muslin fits throughout the body, you'll need to add extra fabric to the shoulders and armhole area. I'm doing this by laying out the flat yoke, front, and back pieces from the original drape from previous spread, since they're already seperated and tested over another muslin layer (shown in green), and drawing in new armhole shapes right on the lower fabric, no paper needed. I start by trimming the front-to-yoke edges to match the proofed upper muslin layer. Next, I shift outward the original armhole and side seam lines, keeping them vertically parallel to the initial drape, and extend the yoke seams to continue outward, with no change to the initial draped angles, as indicated by the solid lines. Then, by following the curve of the original armhole, I add even more upper width by further pivoting the curve (see the dashed red line) for a total increase of about 2 inches (5 cm) at the yoke and 1 inch (2.5 cm) at both sides, front and back. Of course, additions of different amounts can be used.

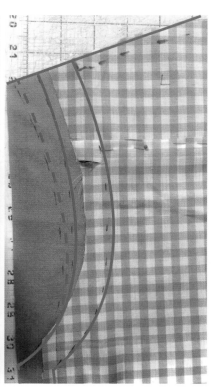

MUSLIN 3:
CREATING EXTENDED ARMHOLES

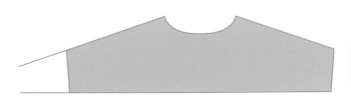

Trace the proofed yoke and make a new pattern for it by extending the ends the same amount as the new muslin fronts and back, as shown in the diagram. Then cut a new yoke from test fabric. Trim the new front and back muslins following the widened side seams and drawn-in, re-angled armholes, as you can see marked on the gingham fronts, below.

Stitch these pieces together, leaving the side seams open, but transfer the markings from the proof muslin at the side seams. Then put the new muslin back on the form. Note that I've cut into the armholes only about half-way down, because with the changes to the total armhole seam length all my extensions created, and with the side-seam changes I'll no doubt add next, I don't know yet where the ends of these curves will eventually wind up. This is also why I allowed no side-seam allowances when cutting new fronts and backs; there is no way I'll need all that extra width when the sides are finished, but I don't yet know exactly how much I might need. But, note that the extra body ease I created at the sides, along with this shoulder-width extension, were both optional for this particular torso form, and would well have been a perfect strategy for providing more body circumference for a form or body that does need it.

Back on the form, I can see that the widened shoulder widths are close to what I'm going for, but the widths at the lower armholes and below are going to need a lot of exploration to both blend into those wide shoulders and not overwhelm the narrow waist. As I experiment with different alignments at the side seams in the first three images, I finally settle, shown on the photo on the bottom right (**A**), on a version which shows repinning the sides with more width taken out in back than in front. This looks good now, but we'll see how it looks when we add the sleeves. I like the way the straight grain along the bottom edge of the front matches the bottom edge of the back.

A

MUSLIN 3: SLEEVE TEST

With the sides roughly pinned, I pinned in the sample sleeves to test those extended shoulders. The left armhole (**L**) is folded under at the wider curve I'd drawn, and the right armhole at the narrower extension. I prefer the full width at the shoulder, and like the way the sleeve falls from either curve, but it's clear there's way too much excess width in back at the armholes and below, on both sides.

In front, it eventually becomes clear that offsetting the edges at the sides doesn't so much pull in the back as make the overall circumference bigger than if I'd simply taken out an equal amount from front and back. I'm still thinking, at this point, that I'll try to keep the side seams about as vertical and nontapered as on the original loose drape, and will take care of the much wider allowances overall on the left side as I repin. And I do notice how the neckline edges are somehow very uneven! No worries, that'll probably be fine when I drape a specific neckline, and be easy to correct as needed when I eventually trace off everything from this muslin to make a final paper pattern.

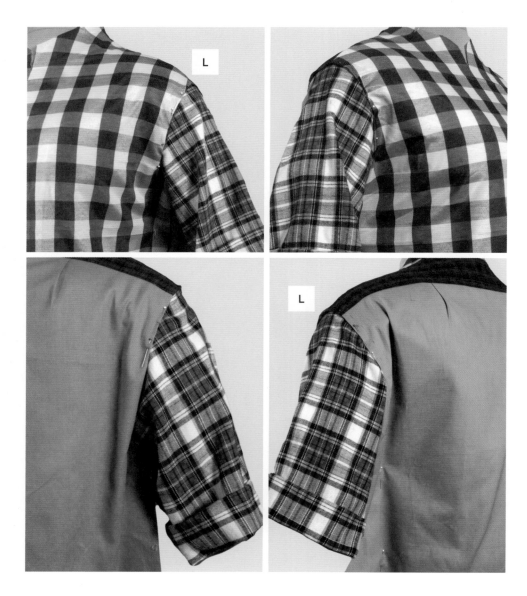

L

MUSLIN 3: SIDE SEAM ADJUSTMENTS

Removing the sleeves allows me to repin the sides. With the side edges realigned on the right side, and before pinning deeply into the seam, everything starts to look better. Note (**A**) how much I've had to raise the back hem in relation to the front to keep the grains square, compared to the same original drape, without extended armholes see (**A**) on page 59. I moved the flexible arm downward to better simulate the relaxed arm position, pressing the side seams into the body as they'd naturally fall on a real body, as described on page 52.

A

I'm pleased with the results on the right side, so far, so I raise the form arms again and experiment with various shapes of the side seams, including how that seam will blend into the armholes at the top. It's becoming clear that some tapering down towards the narrow waist will be the best solution for this muslin, on this form, and yet another example of the power of draping to provide the instant feedback you just can't get with flat manipulations. I decide that the pinned shaping, circled below, is how I'll fix the excess fabric on both sides.

MUSLIN 3: ARMS UP, ARMS DOWN AND NECKLINES

It's particularly critical to test a loose-shoulders drape with arms down, to evaluate how all the extra ease you're building in with the extended armholes will react when pressed against the body, which is what I'm able to simulate on this form, now pinned at right with the same side-seam shaping on both sides. You will want to test this last (hopefully!) test muslin on the wearers if you're not already draping on them.

The smooth back I'm seeing at lower right, untroubled by the compressed-fabric, extra-ease folds at the back armhole curves, with arms down, is exactly the effect I was shooting for, and the tapering is a pleasing discovery and obviously the right thing for this form, even if no doubt better suited to our next topic, the fitted drape!

A

But before we turn to draping fitted shirts, let's finish up with this one. At right, I'm trying out a couple of different neckline shapes (round and dropped in front), seeing with both that while the irregular neck-line allowances I'd noticed earlier aren't in fact interfering with process, the yoke neckline curve in back is too deep and needs to be extended up the neck, to fill in the gap that shows below the paper-tape rings I like to use for this step. I'll just redraw the neck on the yoke pattern to fix this, measuring the gap to find the correct amount.

Once you have an idea about the neckline, it's time to ensure that every pinned or basted seam on this muslin is thoroughly marked both for position and alignment so that wheel-tracings from the muslin, when off the form, will be accurate and complete. I'll start by marking along the lower edge of the neckline ring I prefer.

Once all the seams are traced, the next step is to decide if another proof muslin would be helpful. The only reason I'd do that—rather that going directly to a paper pattern or a fashion-fabric, wearable, test garment— would be if I was troubled by the obvious upper-back asymmetry the existing yoke shape calls attention to at (**A**), which is aggravated by the contrasting fabrics. It would be quite easy to find a less distracting, more nearly horizontal yoke-to-back seam-line curve at the initial yoke-draping stage once you decide that an asymmetrical yoke is worth exploring, so I might be tempted to do that before moving on. But that is up to you.

Either way, my preferred next step would likely be a fashion-fabric test and not a pattern, as discussed on page 31, and as I'll demonstrate in each of the project chapters.

FIT | 4
DRAPING THE FITTED SHIRT

WHAT ARE FITTED SHIRTS?

In this chapter, we explore how to use the drape-to-fit process to create custom-fitted shirt patterns for shirts with these features:

- Increased fitting ease reduction through shaped side seams

- Darts—visible and invisible

- Both fitted and dropped shoulders

- Maximum freedom of movement in the arms and shoulders

- Just enough body ease to drape without wrinkles and follow the shape of the body

Fitted shirts are basically loose shirts made more close fitting in other areas beyond the shoulders. This means we're now going to reshape the body of the draped shirt, instead of merely allowing sufficient straight-sided loose-ness below the armholes to cover the body shapes as smoothly as possible, as was our goal with the loose shirt. And again, once you have the perfectly draped muslin, you want to use to create the paper pattern, download the pdf, "Converting a muslin drape to a paper pattern" at www.quartoknows.com/page/sewing-shirts.

This follows the steps taken in the previous chapter: After molding the yoke and shoulders, leveling the grains front and back, and balancing the sides for a loose fit, we simply take the next obvious step by continuing to pin out any excess ease and smooth out any still-persistent or new wrinkles below the armholes, either at the side or at the yoke seams or within the body pieces where there are no seams.

The difference between reshaping existing seams and where there are no seams is, of course, considerable. Simple as it seems, it can be difficult to match complex body shapes by repinning seams far from where the shaping is actually needed. And as we've just seen in the previous chapter, it can be tricky to try to adjust the fronts to a different degree than the back at the same seam. So, the following photographs demonstrate a unique draping strategy for improving the way we recut side seams, by shaping (reducing the ease) within the body of the back or front.

Pinning out excess where there's no existing seam generally means adding a dart, or something else that reduces the excess fabric, such as gathers, tucks, pleats, or additional seams. Consider any of these as implied options wherever I mention dartmaking in the pages to come, a subject already well covered in many other plac-es. In this chapter, I focus mainly on the far less-explored, and much more shirt-friendly options of eliminating, reducing, or concealing darts while still enjoying all the shaping they so obviously provide.

SIDE-SEAM SHAPING: THE DRAPING WAY

Here's a good example of dart-free, off-seam ease reduction: While pinning right at the side seams to reduce the body ease can certainly work—the last demo in the previous chapter is a good example—better results almost always come from dart-like pinning on the front or back exactly where the excess fabric appears, without reshaping the side seams. This allows shaping the back and front differently and is demonstrated in the photographs, starting with a typical loose drape on form #4.

I started by pinning out the excess fabric. Once pinned out, off-seam ease can certainly be refined into darts. However, the pinned muslin can also be arranged as flat as possible, still pinned, ignoring whatever won't lay flat, and the back (or front) drape can be retraced, including the newly shaped side seams (a result of the ease removal). This transfers the ease reduction back to the seams in a quite useful way, as shown in the photos (**A**, **B**) of new front and back pieces cut from the tracing. There's a limit to how much flat length like this can be removed before the piece becomes too small for the three-dimensional shape, but it is often quite a lot.

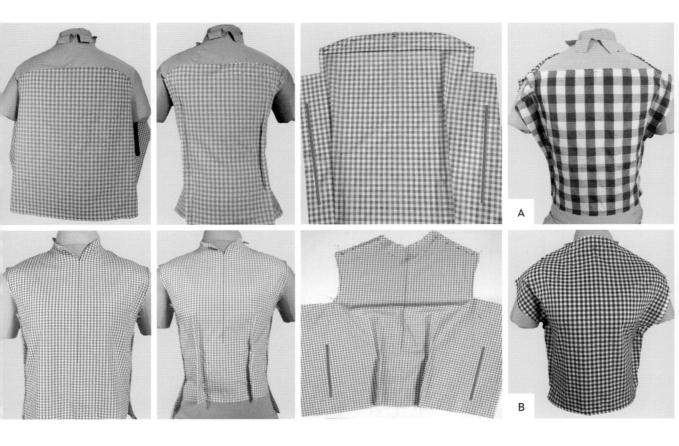

A

B

DARTS: VISIBLE AND INVISIBLE

When draping a fitted shirt on a figure with a bust, a dart-like fold tends to form naturally between the bust point and the nearest part of the armhole as you reduce the ease below the bust at the side seam. This fold is easily pinched and pinned into an actual dart, which has several immediate benefits, as you can see in the photographs at right (**A**, **B**): Once the dart is pinned, the shirt front below the dart smooths right out, and the armhole pulls into a much more suitable shape, however, the armhole is reduced in length by the amount of fabric in the dart folds.

The armhole length reduction is usually an ideal solution for a fitted shirt, especially a fitted shirt that is being developed from a loose one, but if the armhole is already the perfect length or a little more length is still needed afterwards, it can easily be drawn back in, at the top of the side seam, to return it to its original circumference.

Pivoting the dart to another, farther-away edge, to avoid changing the armhole length, is another option, but note in the illustrations below how this increases the length of the dart sides, or legs, making the amount of fabric in the fold between them greater, without adding any increased shaping, since the dart angle doesn't change. The diagrams, below, show two possible and very common alternative placements for the dart and how to make the pattern changes, by slashing and pivoting.

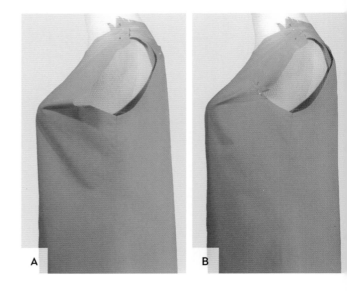

At right, in orange, are the results, in fabric from the dart, pivoting pattern changes shown below. Note that the armholes remain shorter in length and better shaped, but that each dart shift reorients the grain quite dramatically from the bust point to the side seam and at the armhole itself, while the overall body silhouette remains unchanged in the first two examples.

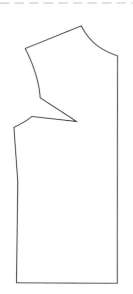

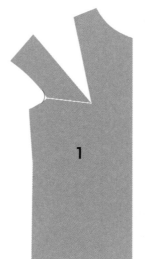
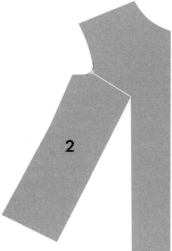

1 Moving the armhole dart to the shoulder.

2 Moving the armhole dart to the hem directly under the bust point.

3 Releasing the shifted-to-bust dart at the hem area.

Note that in example **3**, the below-bust dart has been released (left unstitched), creating a wide, loose fit below the bust, while retaining the dart shaping above and to the side of the bust. The grain shift at the side seam is, of course, unchanged.

A certain amount of this waist ease can be taken up at the side seam to bring the shirt back into trim-fit territory, but the more you pull the front in towards the side seam, the more you'll defeat the purpose of the dart rotation, because this begins to re-create exactly the sort of natural armhole bust dart we started with. With care, you can certainly find useful points of balance, and to some extent, get the best of both worlds. I personally prefer other approaches, as you'll see next.

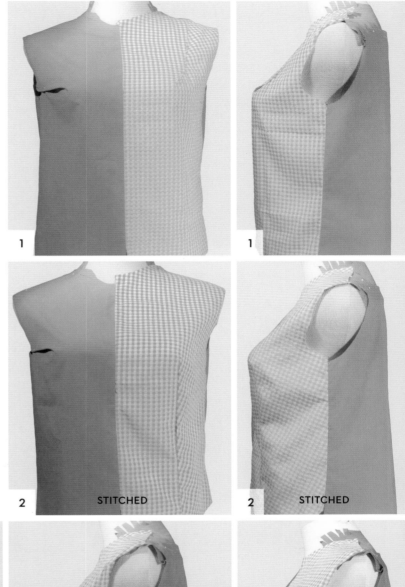

1

1

STITCHED

2

STITCHED

2

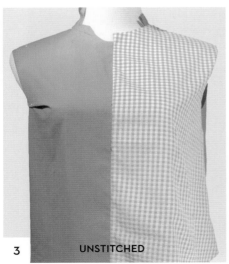

UNSTITCHED

3

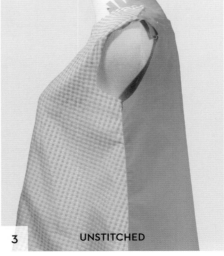

UNSTITCHED

3

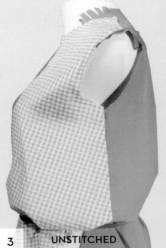

UNSTITCHED

3

FULL GARMENT CONVERSION BY DRAPING

Here's the approach I prefer, rather than dart manipulation: draping for a closer fit. This process begins with a shirt I like, but want to convert from a loose fit to a more fitted shirt. Note that the draping process—for every shirt, regardless the fit—is impacted by the fabric type.

WITH SOFT FABRIC

I start by placing a loose or oversized shirt, with no darts, on form #3. My goal is to pin out as much fabric as I can in the back and side seams without causing new dart folds to appear in the front. This is similar to the side-seam reshaping (within the body of the garment that I did at the beginning of this chapter), but here I'm adding side-seam pinning, for even more ease reduction. As

folds begin to appear at the front armholes, circled below, I stop the ease-reduction pinning through the body.

I believe that these darts folds are small enough that I can drape them away if I use a soft fabric. I trace new front and back body-pattern outlines from the pinned original pieces, laid flat with the pins still in place. I cut the resulting shapes out from a very soft, much-washed flannel sheet, shown at bottom, below.

Back on the form, with the front and back pinned to a yoke traced from the original shirt, the armholes are clearly too wide, but overall the body fit is much better than on the original shirt, and the test muslin can be further draped to fit even better.

It's easy to fix the armhole shaping, and improve the body width as well, by folding, trimming, and repinning the shirt right on the form. You can see how the draped shirt looks smooth and body skimming without any pattern manipulation.

In this process, every seam got further microadjustments, especially at the yoke ends, as I slipped in my trusty sleeve samples. Pinning the sleeves in place

helped confirm that the curve and height of the armhole opening still fit the sleeve and that the front and back of the shirt still looked close fitted without excess fabric. And, there we have it, completely draped armholes on a smoothly fitting, dart-free body—no patterns or gingham squares needed.

WITH CRISP FABRIC

Here's the very same drape, starting with the same shapes—yoke, fronts, and back—as in the previous example, this time cut from fabrics I know to be the exact opposite of the soft flannel I just used—crisp quilting cottons.

These unwashed quilting-cotton solids do not stretch on either grain, yet they don't appear or feel abnormally stiff or unpleasant. They're therefore wonderful for draping muslins when I want to test extreme fabric crispness, by which I mean fabrics that tend to wrinkle in response to even the most subtle excess fabric length or strain, rather than absorb the wrinkles as soft, more flexible fabrics often do.

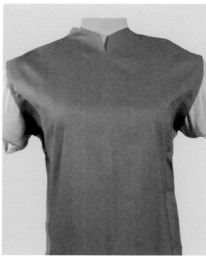

As you can see, even on the same form, I was completely unable to drape away the extra dart-folding length at the front armholes and will have to add darts somewhere in front after all, in order to proceed any further with refining the armholes on these shapes and on this form in such a crisp fabric. A small potential back-armhole dart also appeared, as you can see below, which will probably disappear neatly into a much smaller armhole with continued draping.

But full garment conversion isn't limited to "soft-fabric, no darts" projects alone. They are a wonderfully efficient starting point for any fitted drape, because in one step they capture both the already working parts of any existing shirt, along with rough-draft solutions for all the not-working parts. The photographs at far right show a big, soft shirt on form #2 that needs a little vertical reduction in the back, sides, and at and below the bust, as well as serious help at the shoulders. This is done by lifting and smoothing the fronts upward while bringing the yoke forward and down, pinning them together as needed for an on-grain, dart-free front and sides. The (**A**) images show the shirt before pinning; the (**B**) images show it after pinning, and the bottom two show it flat for tracing. Note how I released the yoke-front pins to lay the front flat, and put in new pins to show where the yoke had been.

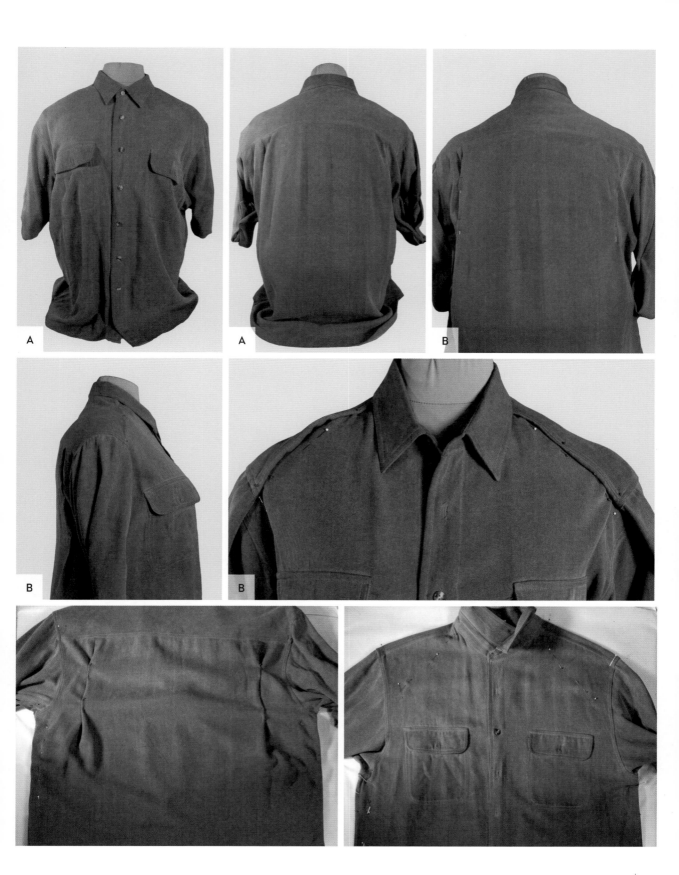

HIDING DARTS IN SEAMS AND UNDER COLLARS

As always, the next step after a full-garment drape is to make a new muslin from the tracings, with extrawide seam allowances, and basted together at the yoke only, which you then put back on the form for further refinement. The source shirt was made from a soft silk twill, but the muslin fabric I've chosen here is crisper, not as extreme as the quilting solids on the previous spread, but more like the fabric already chosen to make project 2 (see page 106). The construction of project 2, a V-neck woman's dress shirt, starts with this finished test muslin.

As you can see, a bit of dartlike folding has reappeared at the front armholes (**A**), most of which I've been able to lift and smooth back into the front-to-yoke seam (**B**). And in back (**C**), there's plenty of excess length at the sides that I was able to easily lift away and hide in the back-to-yoke seam, which neatens up the armhole as well, shortening it without reshaping it.

Still, as I brought the sides closer together for balancing, some bust-dart folding returned with this fabric, and I had to either pin this out as darts or leave the sides alone. Wanting the closer fit at the sides, I decided to try some on-form dart-fold pivoting, since my extra seam allowances would allow that, so I was able to explore various positions along the shoulders, neckline, or even into the center front. Don't be afraid to cut into the center front on the muslin; when you trace the muslin to create the pattern, you can eliminate any openings, or even create a center front opening.

Because project 2 features a V-neckline and a collar I'm hoping to find a place for the darts that might make them easy to conceal under the collar. As we learned from the dart-manipulation demonstrations (page 68), when a dart is pivoted, the shaping it provides (its angle) stays the same, no matter where it's pivoted and no matter how long or short the dart legs need to be to accomplish removing the desired excess fabric.

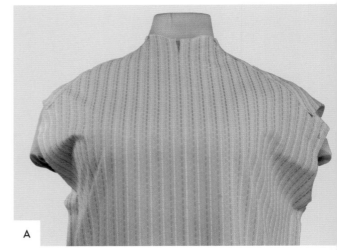

A

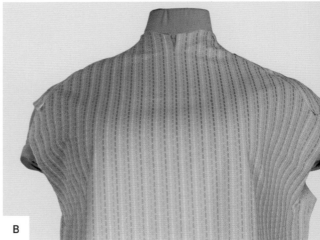

B

C

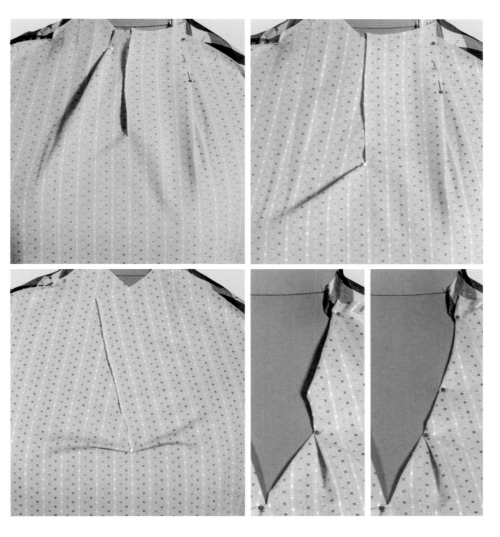

So, for the smallest dart possible, the dart should be pivoted to the seams or edges that are closest to the point. And if we move the darts close to the neckline or into the centerfront, the neckline or center-front details can be designed to conceal these small darts. I settled on the first solution I tried (**A**), as the least fussy. Moving the darts close to the neckline make them easy to cover with a curved collar (**B**) or even to convert to seams, as could be done for any sort of center-front insert shape (**C**).

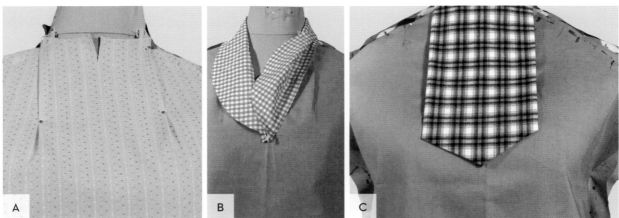

FIT | 5
DRAPING THE TIGHT SHIRT
WHAT ARE TIGHT SHIRTS?

In this chapter, we explore how to use the drape-to-fit process to create custom-fitted shirt patterns for shirts with these features:

- Extreme shaping at side and body seams

- Darts—visible and invisible

- Fitted shoulders

- Optimized, but possible limited freedom of movement in the arms and shoulders

- Minimum body ease, garment follows the shape of the body, possible strain wrinkles

Tight shirts follow the shape of the body everywhere. As with the fitted shirt, the easiest path to greater ease reduction, so that the shirt becomes "tight," is simply to continue pinning ease away from a fitted drape until the muslin is as tight fitting as desired. As before, there are options and variations involved in the drape-to-fit process, including adding body seams, such as "princess" seams. We'll examine these options in the following pages, as I demonstrate how to drape a tightly-fitted shirt. And remember, once you have the perfectly draped muslin, to create the paper pattern, download the pdf, "Converting a muslin drape to a paper pattern" at www.quartoknows.com/page/sewing-shirts.

It's possible you can make a tight-fitting shirt by scaling down an already customized fitted shirt, like the "grading" process used by manufacturers. This means that ease is reduced for every part of the shirt equally, so you would have to take care not to make the sleeves too short (or too tight) or move the neckline too close to the neck.

The most direct path to a customized, tight-fitting shirt might be to start completely from scratch with a customized upper-body drape that makes no effort to be a shirt, but instead create a "ruthless record" of whatever shaping is needed to mimic the upper body so closely as to still be wearable and to allow for movement, but no looser. Then, you could simply add a few classic shirt details to the drape. On the next few pages, I demonstrate how to drape-to-fit a tight-fitting shirt, starting with the fitted drape. Then, I'll share a quick way to drape a tight-fitting body pattern from scratch. (This method also creates a highly accurate custom dress-form cover, ready to pad out to duplicate your identical body shape).

DRAPING A TIGHT-FITTING SHIRT FROM A FITTED TEST MUSLIN

This demonstration begins with the fitted muslin that we last used in the beginning of chapter 4 (on form #4, male with athletic build). In that process, to create a fitted shirt, I repositioned the side seams by pinning out ease in the back, at the location where the extra ease appeared (instead of at the side seams), and traced the still-pinned muslin drape (see page 67) to make a new muslin. Back on the form here, with the side seams basted and armholes trimmed, the shirt muslin looks snug, but there's still plenty of ease to remove from the back and waist, as you can see at the hem (**A**). Here, you can also see a strain wrinkle from chest to side seam. For a fitted shirt, simply releasing the seam near the end of that wrinkle (in other words, allowing extra length) will fix this on this form (**B**). But for a tight fit, that solution won't work because it increases the ease at the release area (**C**). Since I've already taken out about as much ease as the pin-out-and-retrace method can manage, I'll now have to continue with some combination of direct side-seam repinning and dart shaping, both better suited to the more exacting shaping and ease reduction needed here.

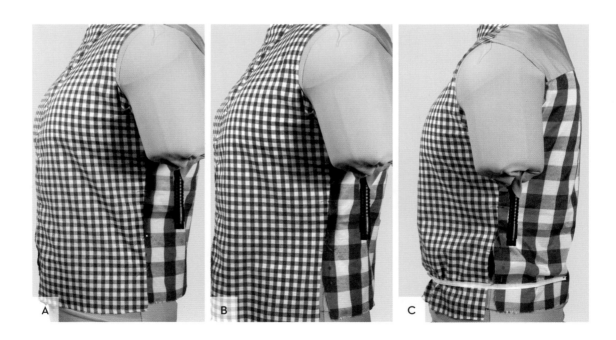

A

B

C

Note: If you are wondering about the black tube-like appendages occasionally seen protruding from the form's arms—these are the part of my home-made form that makes the arms flexible.

The images on this spread document various draped attempts to find the least wrinkled combination of side seam repinning and pinned-out dart shaping in the shirt back as I take the fitted muslin from the previous page into tight territory. They offer another example of how to use draping to manage subtle adjustments that you would never be able to zero in on with flat-pattern adjustments, and how the process itself is one of trial and retrial. I don't say ". . . and error," as judgement and personal preference are always the deciding factors, not "correctness."

The first image with the sides returned to their lowered position shows the muslin as we finished with it on the previous page (**A**).

Note the width and angle of the brown vertical stripe in each subsequent image as I reposition the same folded edge of the blue gingham over the back piece, taking in or letting out ease, with or without back-dart pinning, always looking for the smoothest results in the body and the straightest, most parallel grain lines I can manage at the side seams. Of course, the solutions I'm finding are entirely dependent on the shape of the form, so it is important to remember that different body shapes will require different pinning and repinning.

Images (**B**) and (**C**) show my finished test drape and the side seams I settled on. I left a little diagonal strain from the chest on each side and moderate looseness in the center back, deciding that, in this case, I preferred this to perfect smoothness. The next step is to take the muslin off the form and trace it for what I expect will be the final muslin.

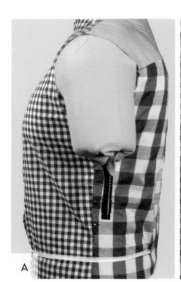

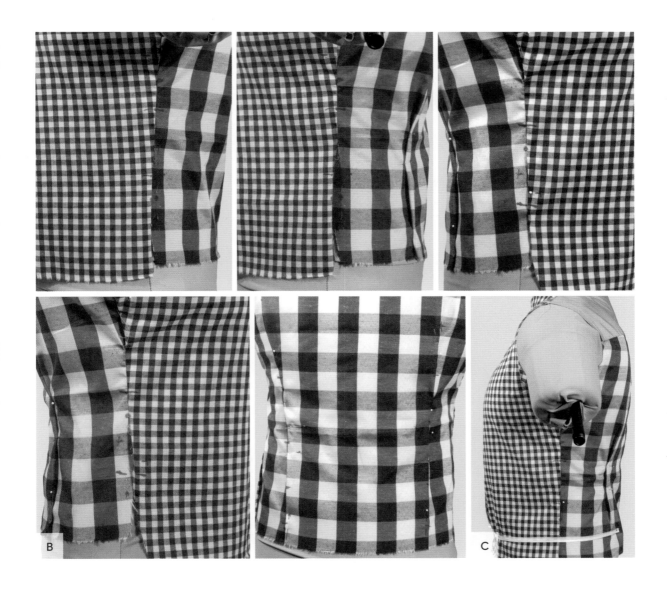

Here's the new version of the earlier drape from the previous page, with the back pinning converted to symmetrical seams rather than darts, although darts would have been equally effective, but not as suitable or as attractive for the specific project I have in mind (see project 4, page 126). I also created a center front opening for the front of this drape. No doubt I should just own up to basically disliking darts on shirts, in general, and accept this as mere prejudice. I have no intention of trying to

infect others with dart dislike; please go ahead and use darts if you like them! And, rejoice with me in recognizing how personal taste is an essential aspect of your designer's vision.

I cut the new muslin fronts with an overlapping opening because project 4, which is made from this tight-fitting drape, has a center front opening and because I thought I might need asymmetrical adjustments to the front pieces. Notice that in the upper-right chest area, I've

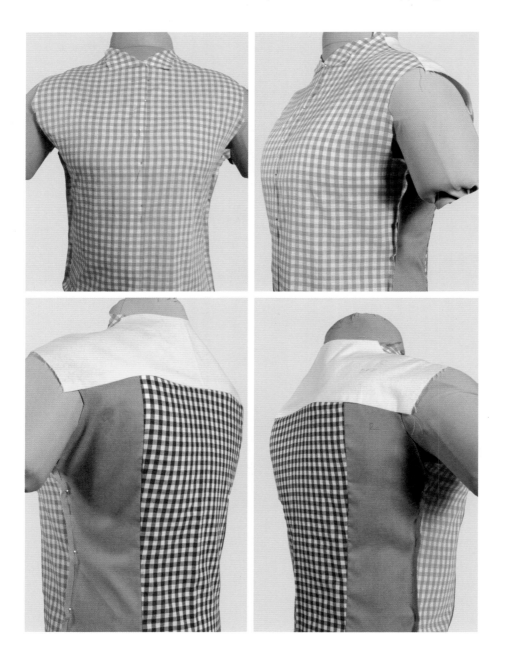

pinned away a little ease at the exact location where the excess fabric appears (only on the right side) and redrew the armhole (**A**). I traced the pinned right front drape (**B**). To test the new fronts, I made another test muslin; see how much better the armhole fits now (**C**). When creating the final front patterns, it will be important to mark right front and left front, since they are different, as they are on almost all draped patterns.

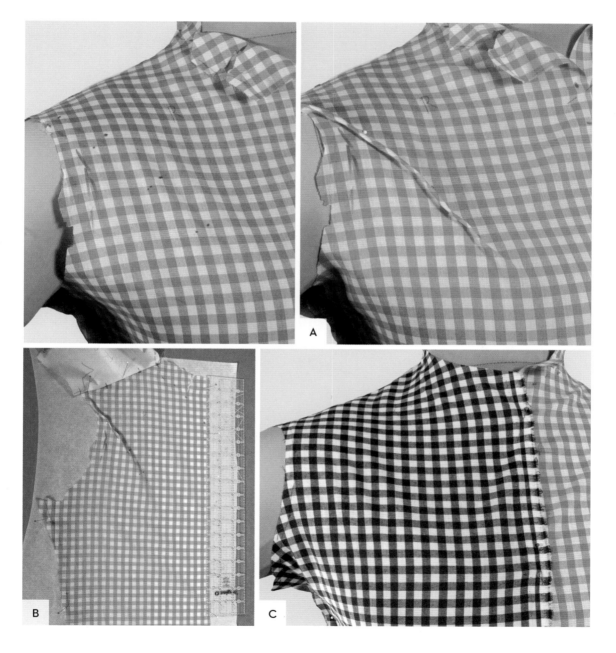

CONVERTING DART SHAPING TO SEAMS FOR A TIGHT-FITTING SHIRT

As we've seen, the closer we bring basic shirt shapes in towards the body, the more likely we are to create excess dart folding, in all the expected places, front and back, at the bust, shoulders, shoulder blades, and the waist and hips below the chest.

A very helpful and commonly used shirt-design tactic is to convert these folding excesses of fabric into seams rather than darts as I did on the previous pages. This is the same thing we automatically did when the yoke and back seam line curved near the armholes; that excess fabric could have been turned into shoulder darts, but we were able to transfer the excess fabric into the back/yoke seam and thereby cause it to disappear (see page 38).

Additional seaming through the area where the darts end, and where the dart fullness can be pivoted, results in princess seams. The princess seam is a useful way to eliminate excess ease for both men and women who want a little more structure than a dart would provide on a sculpted garment.

The series of diagrams, below, shows how to convert a bust dart and a lower dart into a seam from hem to armhole; this can be done in the garment front and by the same method in the garment back. Remember though, from chapter 4, page 68, you can pivot, the upper front dart anywhere around the bust point and still blend it into the below-bust dart, or you can pivot the below-bust dart elsewhere, but it is usually left where it appears in the diagram. This is typical flat pattern-making dart manipulation (for more information, see the downloadable pdf for "Dart manipulation").

You can sew a standard seam here, but to form the seam and clean finish it at the same time, it is a good idea to use a two-pass flat-felled seam. These seams can be tricky to sew on tight curves. Take note of the final illustration, which shows how a flat-felled seam requires uneven seam allowances, and on which side to put the wider one for typical results. Flat-felled seams are described in detail in the downloadable pdf, "Flat-felled seam."

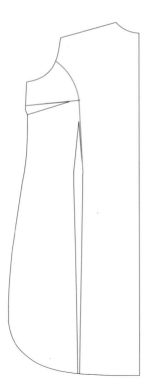
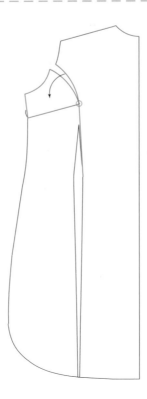
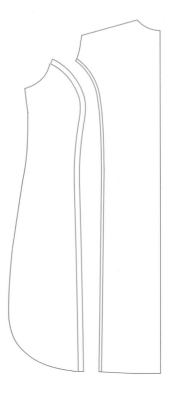

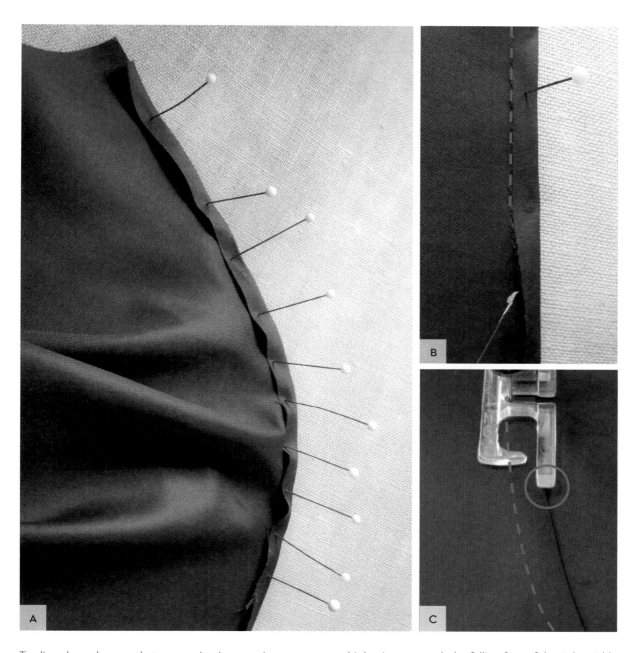

To align shaped seams that are curving in opposite directions when layered for stitching, it can be very helpful to pin them onto a padded surface both as they're brought into alignment and as you prefold the wider allowance over the narrower one (**A**). Tiny dabs of glue stick on the point of a pin, as shown at top right, perfectly secure the arrangement and folds when the pins are removed for stitching (**B**).

Such curves are, with some fabrics, easier to handle with a felling foot (**C**), but even if this proves challenging and

multiple pins are needed, a felling foot of the right width can still be the perfect tool for edge-guiding both the first and second pass the seam requires, as indicated by the dashed lines. Note that the point at which any curve must align with the foot is directly opposite the needle, here, it's offset to the left to create the required width, not at the front of the foot, which sometimes needs to ride over the edge as it does here (**circled**), for the edge to be perfectly placed when it gets to the needle.

FOIL WRAPPING FOR BODY CLONING

Here's that promised alternative technique for developing a "ruthless record" of any body shape, from the neck down, torso or full length! (I've made several torso forms, through to the hips, but that's all I've tried, so far!) This body-cloning technique is not specific to making shirts, and it could certainly be useful in pattern-making for very tight-fitting garments, since it results in a complete pattern collection for making a skin-tight, body-molded fabric garment.

The idea is, to first wrap the "victim" or "volunteer" as snuggly as possible in foil, holding the loose pieces in place with light taping as you mold the layers. Then you secure the molded layers with wider and stronger clear tape, applied liberally so there are no loose foil edges. You'll also see I've molded the foil over onto the arms a little so I can draw in an armhole, but I've yet to find these armlet pieces useful after cutting them off to define a clear armhole, and I eventually toss them, perhaps prematurely.

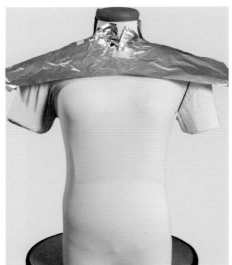

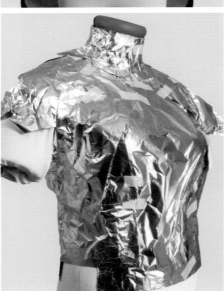

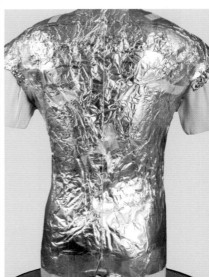

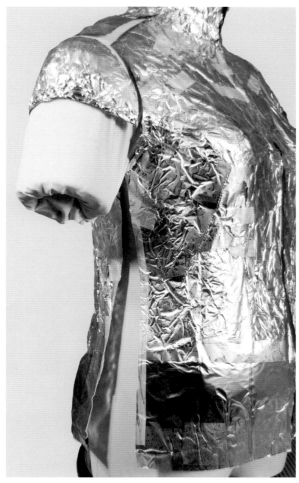

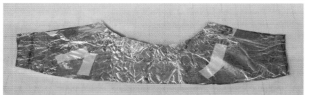

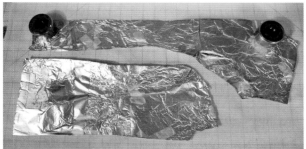

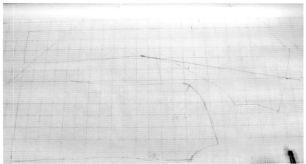

Use a marker to indicate basic pattern lines, but you don't want the marker to poke through the foil, so make sure the tape completely covers any areas to be marked. Some people use plastic wrap instead of foil, but I find foil much lighter, cooler, and less suffocating, as well as easier to mold without overcompressing, and faster, too.

Once wrapped and taped, the next step is to mark cutting lines on the body clone. The marks should be made just where you'd expect to find seams on a similarly tight garment or basic fitting shell; that is, at vertical centers, using a plum line to mark vertical center; directly across points of maximum protrusion as where princess seams would go; around the neck and arms where necklines and armholes would naturally fall; and along the shoulders. For shirt-making purposes, I suggest drawing in yoke seams, as I've done in these photos.

Once you've marked the foil clone, cut it off the body along the marked lines and then flatten the pieces for tracing, eliminating the less-dramatic three-dimensional curves. It's relatively easy at any stage to change design lines; for instance, if you decide you don't want armhole princess seams, simply tape the pieces back together and redraw the seam to go to the shoulder. Trace the foil pieces onto pattern paper, carefully marking alignment points across matching pieces, but don't attempt to true any of the seamlines you've just so carefully captured; use them exactly as is. You'll refine them during the next step.

With the patterns made from traced the foil pieces, I always cut muslin pieces to make a test drape. To make a wearable garment from a foil wrap, you'll very likely need to add ease, not pin more out, especially below the arms. This is most easily done by pinning the muslin tests more loosely at the side seams if these are cut with extrawide allowances, but can also be done at any other seam, including the center front.

To make a form cover instead of a test muslin, baste the front, back, and yoke together, and then proceed to our usual ease-reduction pinching-out where needed (here it's across the yoke and at the side bust, both sides),

followed by more tracing to capture all the further reduced pieces. Then, of course, you will want make a new muslin test, shown at the bottom center and right.

For my purposes, I have only used these foil patterns to make form covers to slip over a smaller form and then pad out to make a perfect torso form, duplicating the exact body shape of the volunteer you wrapped. Or even better, use the test muslin as the shell, inside of which you build up the form itself, assuming you don't already have a form it'll fit over without distorting—which if you've got anything but picture-perfect posture is quite unlikely.

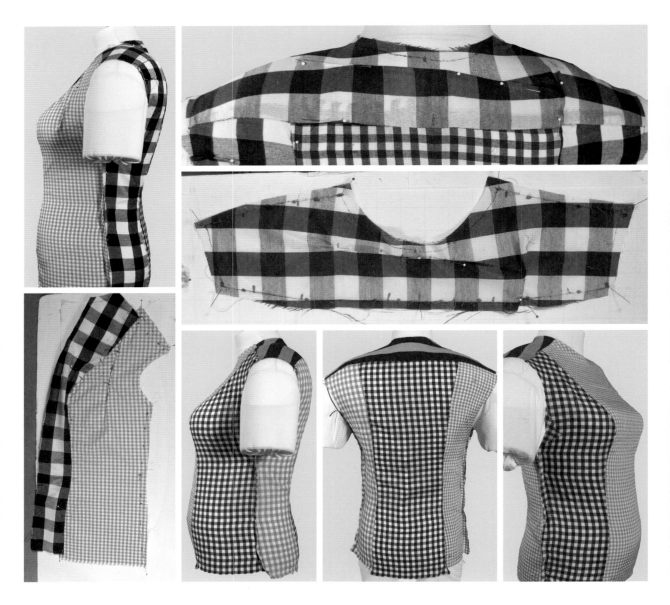

MAKING A FORM FROM A FOIL WRAP

It's a lot easier than it may appear to go from foil wrap pattern to a form like this one. As you can see, I made the final muslin out of actual muslin, with a center-front separating zipper, which certainly simplified the foam-stuffing part of the process. There's a more detailed account of the whole process at my blog, including a list of a few helpful tools.

A key feature of the finished form is the second cover, made from a smooth and somewhat slippery dancer's leotard stretch knit, also listed at the blog, which not only makes the cover presentable, but very usefully smooths out the angularity of the rough-cut foam inside. This second cover was not made from a pattern, it was just roughly shaped and stretched to fit. The soft, pinable lightness of the finished form is a blessing, compared to any other forms I've used, so what started as a quick-and-dirty form project has turned into my first choice, form-making method, since these forms are so pleasant to work with, and so easy to store. They're more like pillows than furniture!

The hard—well, harder—part of the whole project is the slow, future refining of your form so it really does help with fitting and draping. This doesn't mean necessarily that the form needs to become more exactly like the body it serves, but it does mean you will need to adapt the form to your fit-to-drape process, so that the garments you drape on it come out as you wish. For example, if there's a level of ease reduction that you're rarely going to want to exceed, the most useful thing your form can do is to match that, not your no-ease shape. But whatever you want from it, your dress-making clone will very likely need to be massaged over time. Details at the blog!

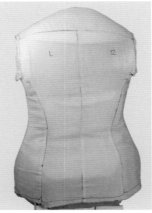
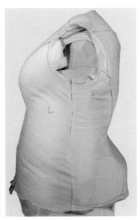

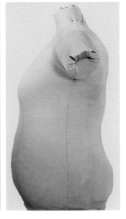

SEW | PROJECTS
BASIC SHIRT CONSTRUCTION
THE SEQUENCE

The diagrams on these pages provide a quick overview of the most basic sequence of steps typically used to put together the most basic sort of shirt, with a plug at far right for inserting sleeves after the side seams and underarms are complete, instead of flat. Obviously, there is an enormous range of different construction sequences that different garment details and finishes require, several of which you'll see in the following projects, and many of which are covered in detail in the two previous books I've written that are entirely about shirt construction, with very little on fitting (see Resources). The point of these diagrams is to make sure that all readers, including those who may have never made a shirt, have the same baseline introductory look at the process. Be sure to check out the downloadable pdf's www.quartoknows.com/page/sewing-shirts for more construction detail on the following projects and making shirts in general.

The logic here, as with most sewing projects, is to join all the smaller garment pieces, like pockets, cuffs, and bands, to the large main pieces while they're still unconnected to other large pieces and are as easy to handle as possible.

The first step before joining either the fronts or back to the yoke layers is to add details to the fronts and back.

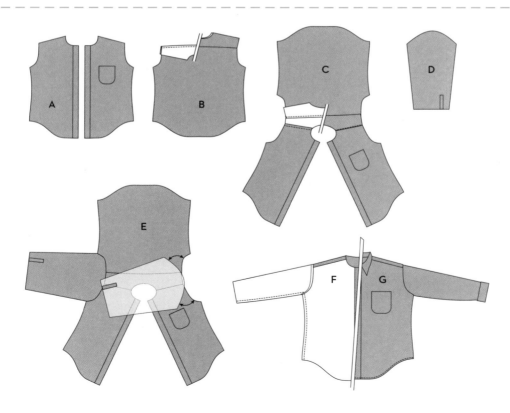

1. Add pockets and front bands (**A**) to the front; complete any pleats, tucks, or gathers you may want at the back-to-yoke seam.

2. Attach the yoke to the back next (**B**), sandwiching the back between the inner and outer yoke layers in one seam and then pressing all the layers forward.

3. Next, join the fronts to the inner yoke layer only (**C**), and press these seams towards the yoke. The front edges of the upper yoke layer should be pressed to precisely cover each seam line, so edge-stitching along these edges can both close the yoke and conceal the seams beneath.

4. Construct the plackets and sew them on the sleeves (**D**); then attach the sleeves (**E**) before stitching the side and underarm seams.

5. Stitch the underarm and side seams all in one pass (**F**).

6. Finish by attaching the collar, cuffs, and hemming the shirt (**G**). The collar could also have been added before the sleeves.

The most common variation to this sequence comes from different collar types, some of which are layered between the yokes, and different hem shapes, some of which need to be finished at the same time as the side seams.

The diagrams, below left, show the common method for attaching cuffs and collars (or stands). These garment details are double layers, so, to start, you need to pre-fold the seam allowance of the inner layer to the wrong side along the edge that joins to the shirt or sleeve body, then sew the outer layers with right sides together with the garment edges. This makes it easy, once the piece is turned right side out and joined to the sleeve or shirt, to tuck the seam allowances inside and edge finish or hand stitch the piece closed.

The remaining sequence of diagrams shows how sleeves are inserted as tubes, not flat, as on the previous page. Turn the garment inside out and the sleeve right-side out, either with the raw edges matched as shown, or extended evenly to allow for joining with a flat-felled seam. Note, that this method of inserting a sleeve makes it much easier to adjust both the rotational alignment and the comparative lengths as you pin two already circular seams together, than to guess at how two linear seams might be similarly shifted before they're turned into circles.

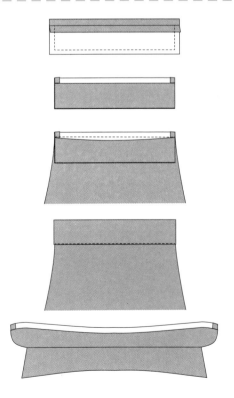

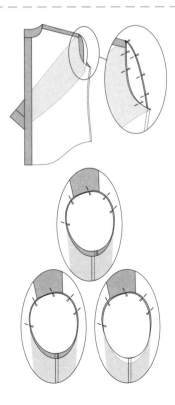

LOOSE, LINED SHIRT JACKET

This loose-fitting, lined, shirt-style jacket may appear to be a complex project, but it's no more complicated than the basic shells we draped in the first half of this book, with no more extraordinary features beyond the shirts described in What's a Shirt? (see page 8).

DRAPING FOR OUTERWEAR FIT

The inspiration for this project comes from the vintage Pendleton 49er shirt-jacket shown below on form #1. You can see the original garment doesn't fit the form well, so I need to drape a test muslin to create a pattern or to correct the pattern I traced from the original, as described in the downloadable pdf, "Converting a Muslin drape to a paper pattern."

CONSTRUCTION SEQUENCE

For detailed, how-to construction steps, refer to the downloaded pdf, "Construction of the Loose-Fitting Shirt Jacket."

1. Outer-layer fronts and back joined to outer yoke layer
2. Front facings joined to front lining, then inner fronts and back joined to inner yoke layer
3. Layers joined at front only
4. Collar added
5. Inner sleeves added to inner layer, then inner side seams joined
6. Outer layer side seams joined, then outer sleeves added
7. Layers joined at hems as hems are finished
8. Buttons and buttonholes added.

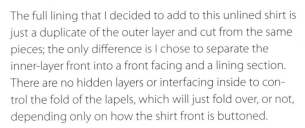

The full lining that I decided to add to this unlined shirt is just a duplicate of the outer layer and cut from the same pieces; the only difference is I chose to separate the inner-layer front into a front facing and a lining section. There are no hidden layers or interfacing inside to control the fold of the lapels, which will just fold over, or not, depending only on how the shirt front is buttoned.

The most interesting challenge of this project from a drape-to-fit perspective, is how to drape it so the fit is not just loose, but loose even when worn as outerwear over other loose layers. The secret is to pad the form with an additional layer (or multiple layers, if needed); done by dressing the form in a typical garment or layers that you might wear under the shirt jacket. I added two padding garments and chose the thinner, more slippery one to go on last to help prevent the draping project from hanging up on the heavier, fuzzier, garment I put on first.

Here's the original jacket back on the padded form, and it already looks better, in front anyway. Because the form doesn't have arms, I can use the sleeves of the padding shirts as extra padding, instead of sliding them in the arms of the shirt jacket. And the sleeves fall right where I need the extra padding, along the side seams.

Seeing how nicely the padding filled out the jacket, I draped my first test on the padded form, again with the extra padding sleeves hanging inside, not outside, of the armhole.

Knowing the asymmetry of this particular form (because it represents my body), I allowed extra fabric so the front muslin could be a bit wider to allow for a likely shift outward of the yoke width, and initially marked a front armhole to match (**A**).

Since the test drape now has the extra ease I need (from the padding shirts), I was able to remove the padding layers and proceed, knowing the extra ease they provided is now already built into the patterns I'll be working with from this drape forward.

You can see a strain wrinkle forming from the low mid-chest area to my left shoulder (**B**), and the same thing, although less distinct, going toward the right shoulder. These are long familiar issues for my forward-shoulders posture, which tend to deform the front armhole curves forward just as they come into the yoke ends.

A

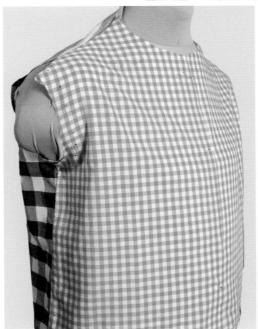

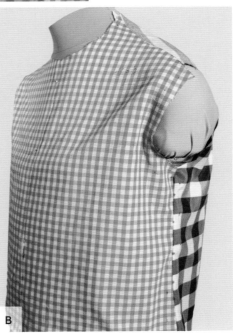

B

REFINING THE YOKE

To address this upper-chest wrinkle, I added length to the armhole curve at the front-to-yoke seam, by pulling more seam allowance into the seam from under the muslin where it crosses my knobby shoulder (**A**).

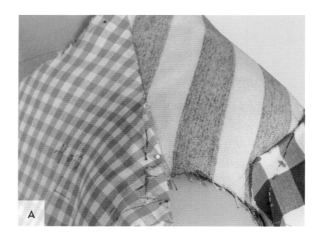

A

Once I was satisfied with the fit of the light cotton muslin, the next step was to trace the muslin and recut it in wool fabric to better evaluate how the actual garment would eventually work in a much heavier fabric. The yoke came first, and you can see the chalk lines I've drawn on it to address my first concern, the dramatic back curve that would need to match that deeply curved yoke-to-back edge (**B**). I decided that I'd rather reshape the yoke edge (no plaids or stripes in the garment fabric to make this too obvious) than straighten out the back.

The problem was that a straight line cut across the entire yoke width would result in yoke ends that were very different widths, given the asymmetry of my shoulder blades. The chalkline in the images shows how I finally determined to redraw the edge, with different width yoke ends at the expense of a straight seam (**C**) and (**D**). In retrospect, I'd certainly acknowledge that it might be wiser to favor a straight yoke seam, since a curved seam might be more noticeable than two different width yoke ends that that would never be seen together. Next time . . .

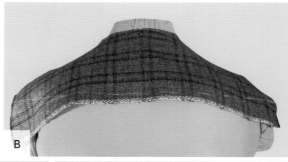

B

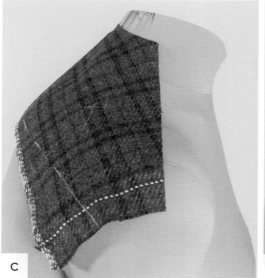

C

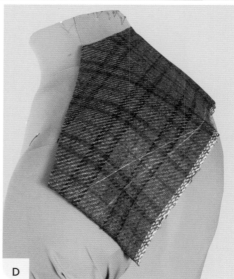

D

REDRAPING IN WOOL PRACTICE FABRIC

Now that I am working with these heavy nonraveling test fabrics, I decide that I can eliminate a difficult tracing step by trimming away the wool seam allowances. It is much easier to mark the fabric against a heavy cut edge than to try to trace through it, and I could possibly use this wool yoke muslin as a pattern guide. The chalk marking on the wool was frustrating because it brushed off too quickly, making it difficult to be precise. You can see how I started marking the seam lines in the circled details below, starting with the trimmed-off front seam

allowances on the yoke. I continued carefully trimming the wool pieces exactly at the seam lines, at the armholes, and across the yoke ends at each armhole; I marked the side seam lines (didn't trim the extra fabric away), since I would continue to adjust the side seams in future steps.

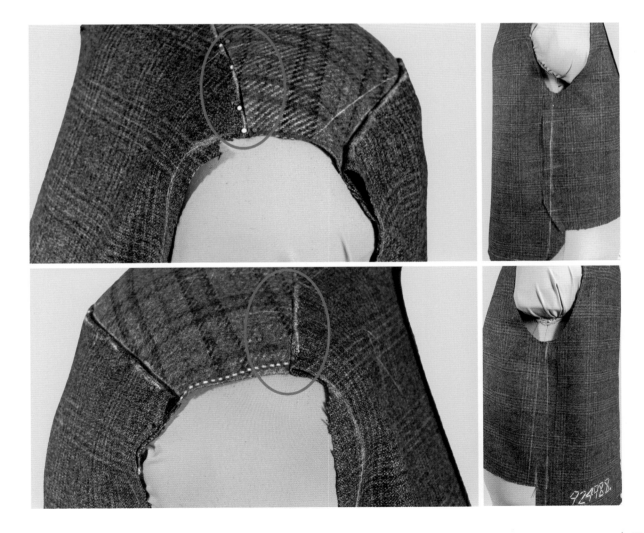

TURNING PARTIAL DRAPES INTO FULL PAPER PATTERNS

Below are the asymmetrical, trimmed woolen partial-muslin fronts and back pieces aligned at the centers with the right side of the fabric carefully marked (since it is difficult to determine right/wrong sides of this particular fabric) and the right and left sides also marked. If your front drape is symmetrical there is no need to cut both a right and left side, since they will be identical (**A**).

Also shown is the original traced front, with the facing shape copied from the source shirt-jacket, the inspiration for this project (**B**).

To trace the draped pieces (which I know fit well), I've positioned the still-aligned front pattern drapes against the original tracing (the one from the source shirt), using the centers and the shoulder seams to orient them. Circled on that image you can, I hope, make out the double layers of tracing paper I've slipped under the matched muslins and traced pattern (**C**).

The next image (**D**) shows the two tracing-wheel-marked outlines I made onto those tracing-paper layers, one of each front aligned only at the front edge, which is the same on both fronts, and marked with red dashes. The differences between the two tracings are along the shoulder, neck, and armhole (where the asymmetries fall).

The bottom photo (**E**) shows, in red dashes, the same partially asymmetrical front pattern retraced to create separate patterns for the front facings and their identical lining inserts, again on doubled tracing layers so there will be one tracing for each of the asymmetrical facings.

At last, I'm ready to cut out the fashion fabrics.

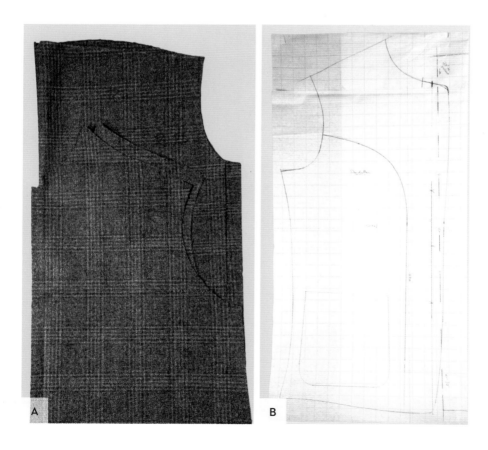

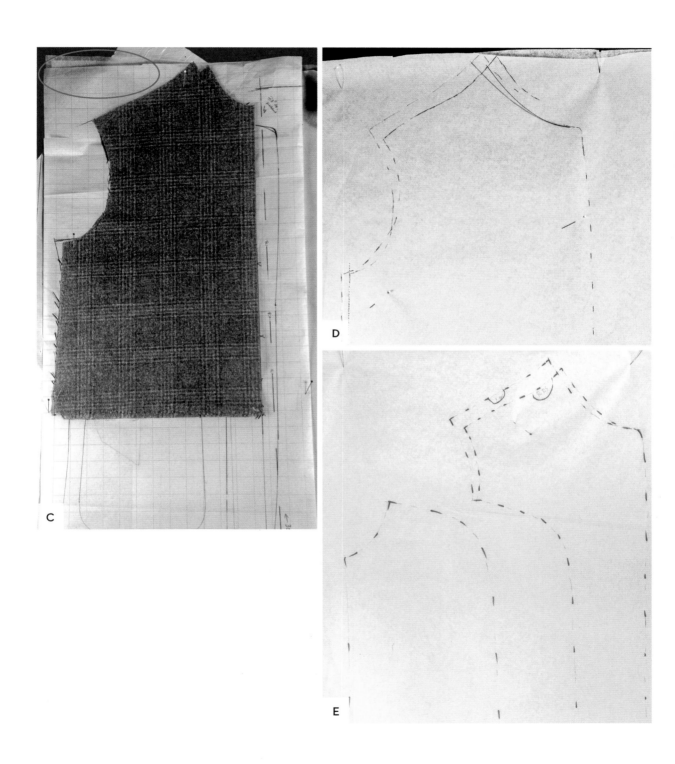

C

D

E

SEWING YOKES TO OUTER AND LINING LAYERS OF FASHION FABRIC

Refer to the downloadable pdf, "Converting a muslin drape to a paper pattern" to confirm where and how to add seam allowances to the patterns, including the test-fabric yoke.

Right before cutting the outer layers of the shirt jacket (fronts, back, and yoke) from the fashion fabric, I decided I'd better thread-mark (since the chalk rubs off) the full front-edge stitching line (**A**), the start of the neckline, and the front armhole on each side (**B**). This way, I didn't need to precision-cut those seam allowances since I had clear stitching guide lines and would be trimming the excess fabric away anyway. I did cut precise seam allowances for the already carefully fitted yoke and the edges joining them, but I allowed generous, rough seam allowances to all the edges below the armholes, knowing

I'd need to be able to adjust them as I progressed with the actual fabrics. The yoke end in the middle image is longer than the front because I cut the yoke symmetrically, and the fronts and my shoulders are not symmetric, resulting in the uneven armhole curve that will need to be fixed.

Next, I joined each layer's yoke to its respective front and back, after assembling the front facings with their respective lining pieces (**C**), taking great care to recall that right side out was different for each layer! I then tried both layers on the form, individually and then together, with side-seam pinning tests each time, to see how the outer layer and the lining were working together.

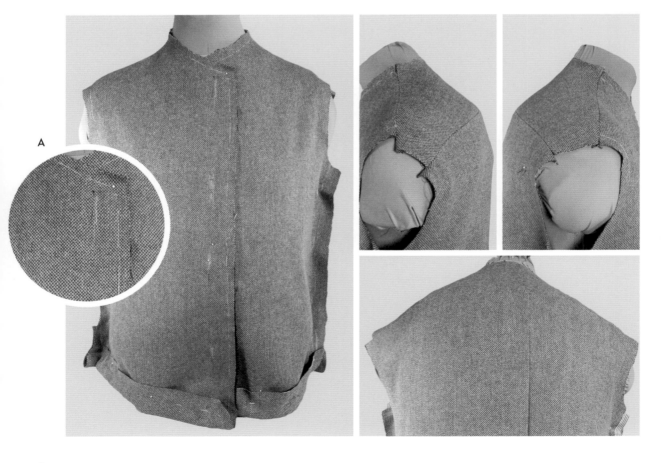

A

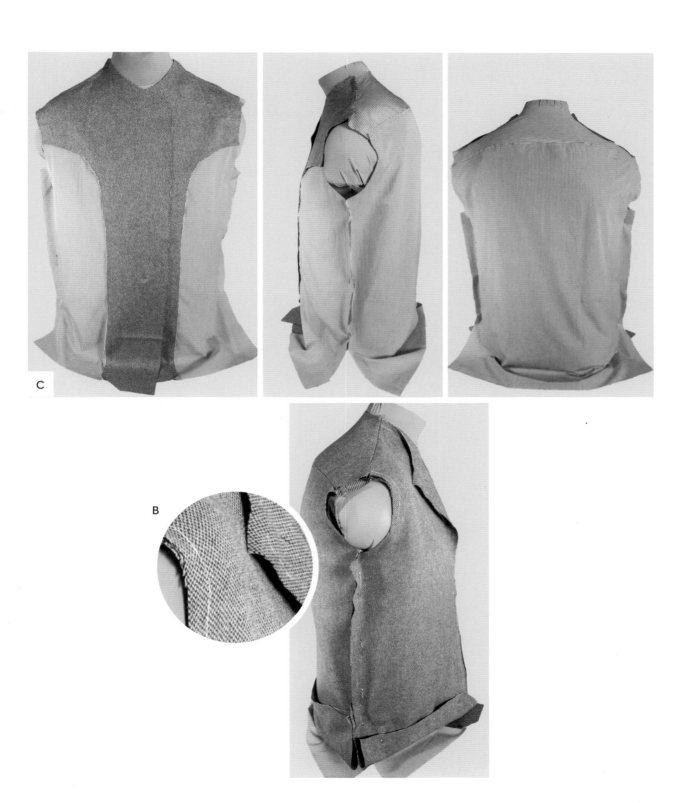

C

B

JOINING FRONT EDGES

Next up is finishing the front edges by sewing the facing to the garment front, with right sides together, starting from the facing's width at the hem, around the hem curve (taken from the original garment) at the bottom, following the basting along the slightly curved edge, up to the most critical little curve (which is not a pivoted corner and which has to exactly match its opposite—careful marking and slow stitching!) where the front becomes the neckline, then onto the marked points where the two neckline seams would flip out to be joined together inside the collar layers. The little red mark on my form's neck is, of course, the center.

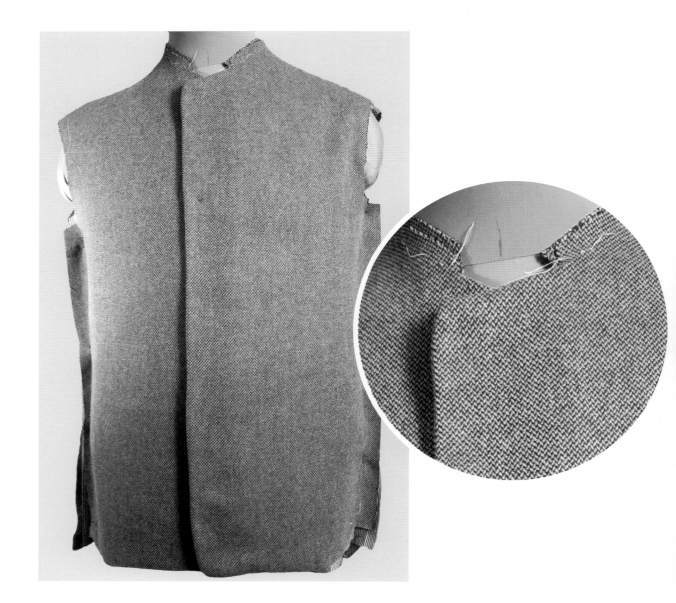

TESTING COLLAR PATTERNS

I made a tracing of the original shirt jacket's rather too-pointed collar, for my taste anyway (**A**), and a drawing (**B**) of a collar with ends long enough so they could easily overlap and button across my neck when the fronts were fully buttoned up. I created this collar pattern by basting a variety of single-layer heavier-muslin sample shapes to the collar allowances on the form and

fiddling with them, as shown. The three images of different shaped collars in muslin tests didn't make the cut, because I didn't like their straight seam line at the neck edge, unlike the curve I'd borrowed from the original shirt jacket for the rather odd, but doing-its-job winning design.

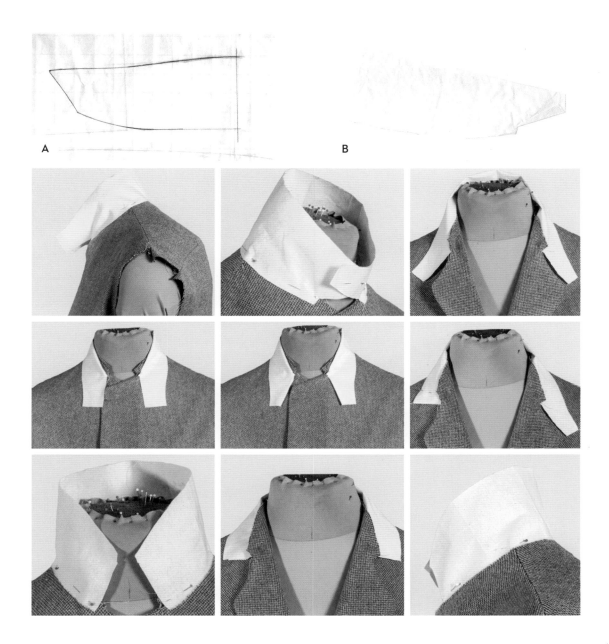

A

B

MAKING AND JOINING THE COLLAR

I'd been saving an old pair of corduroy trousers with a ripped-out back pocket (*not* made by me!) to swipe some of its nicely colored fabric, and this was just the opportunity for which I'd been waiting. And, as you'll see in better detail in project 4, I'm currently on a "wrap, don't turn corners" kick, so that's the method I chose to use to make this collar. The idea is to cut the under-collar fabric and any interfacing (here, I used a simple muslin layer, same fabric as the test collar as interfacing) exactly at the outer collar seam lines, and only the outer collar layer with seam allowance (the seam allowance should be approximately twice the width necessary to fold neatly around the other layers; a test collar is required). This wrapping of the extrawide seam allowance on the outer collar is done in exactly the way described for princess-seam edges prep (see page 83), except the raw edge is folded under. Top- and/or edge-stitching holds the wrapped layers down. Fast, clean, and a-typical, what's not to like? The inner collar layers get joined to the neck line—ends carefully positioned—just like a standard collar, and the woolen under-collar (nonraveling and bias cut in this case) edge is closely hand-whipped over the seam (**A**) to close it all up. For more step-by-step details, refer to the downloaded pdf, "Construction of the Loose-Fitting Shirt Jacket."

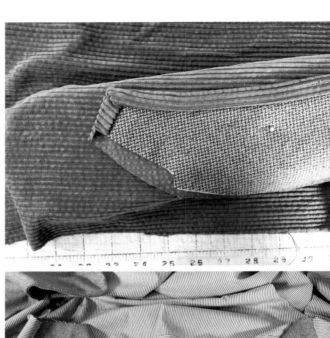

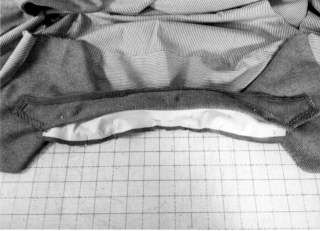

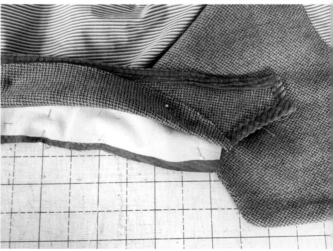

A

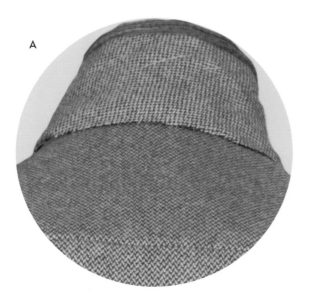

SEWING THE SIDE SEAMS AND BASTING THE UPPER NOTCH

At this point, the outer layer and the lining are joined only at the front edges and around the neckline, and will stay this way until the final hemming, when they'll get a few strategic tackings, to secure the lining sleeves to the outer layer at the armholes and perhaps a few actual joined edges along the hem or side seams; I am not sure yet. Sometimes, linings hang more smoothly if left separate at the hems.

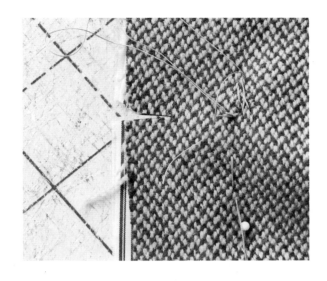

It's time to try on the partially finished garment, so I pin all the sides together separately, on the form, to smooth the layers to each other, mark the positions with a single clip, and then take a few strong, looping basting stitches right at the top of each side seam through all the layers . . . and slip it on for the first time. . . . Ah, it's working!

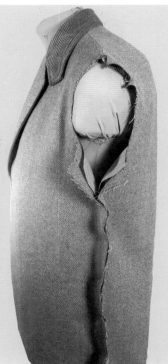
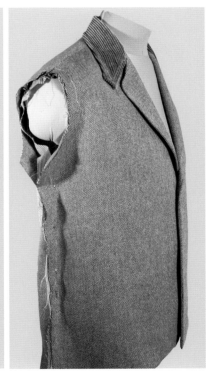

ADDING SLEEVES

Because the outer layer and lining layer are still easily separated, it's also easy to add the sleeves, once again taking care to keep wrong sides together. I choose to join the lining layer's sleeves flat, so I can sew the sides and underarm seams in one long seam. Then, for the outer layer, I insert the sleeves in-the-round, after closing the side and underarm seams. I've used the sleeve pattern traced from the original garment, and the armhole curves, which were slightly altered during the initial draping (but remember, I trimmed the armhole curves in the wool-draping step so they're already the correct shape). Refer to "Pin- and Wheel-Tracing" on page 26.

So, all looks good, and now the added benefits of a lining appear: I get to forgo any armhole seam finishing, and even get to press the outer layer's seam allowances towards the sleeve, which looks more jacket-like than towards the body would.

And here I stopped.

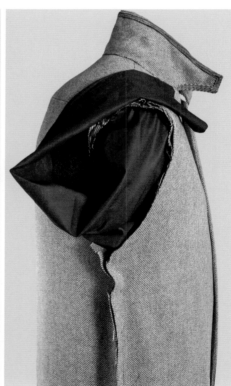

READY FOR FINISHING

The remaining finishing steps, including a decision on outer-layer pockets—and buttonholes—will take much more time than I've got before I need to submit this book! Much to think about—at my leisure! Refer to the downloaded pdf, "Construction of the Loose-Fitting Shirt Jacket," and to my blog for more finishing touches.

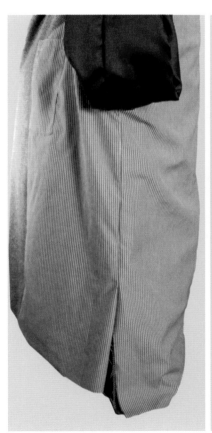

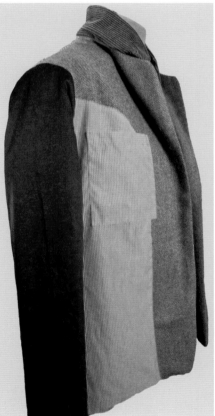

PROJECT
2

FITTED V-NECK DRESS SHIRT

The muslin for this project was originally draped on form #2 (see page 74), and as you'll recall it was a fitted shirt with neckline darts, which we will now transform into a dress shirt with the darts hidden behind a V-neck collar.

Starting with the finished drape, I added extra width on the back-draping piece to allow for a small tuck on each side of the yoke (**A**). I positioned the tucks close to the sides to provide extra ease the entire length of the shirt, allowing deeper pin-outs through the waist area and more flexible shaping options. Notice how I was able to remove excess ease at the center back (**B**). And, those folds at the front neckline are ready for their dart conversion!

CONSTRUCTION SEQUENCE

For detailed, how-to construction steps, refer to the downloaded pdf, "Construction of the Fitted V-Neck Dress Shirt."

1. Fronts joined to outer yoke layer
2. Front darts created at neckline
3. Collar made, then joined to neck between yoke layers and neckline facings and fronts
4. Back darts and tucks stitched, then back-joined to yoke layers
5. Front closures added with front facings
6. Side seams joined
7. Sleeves added
8. Cuffs, side vents, and hems finished
9. Buttons added

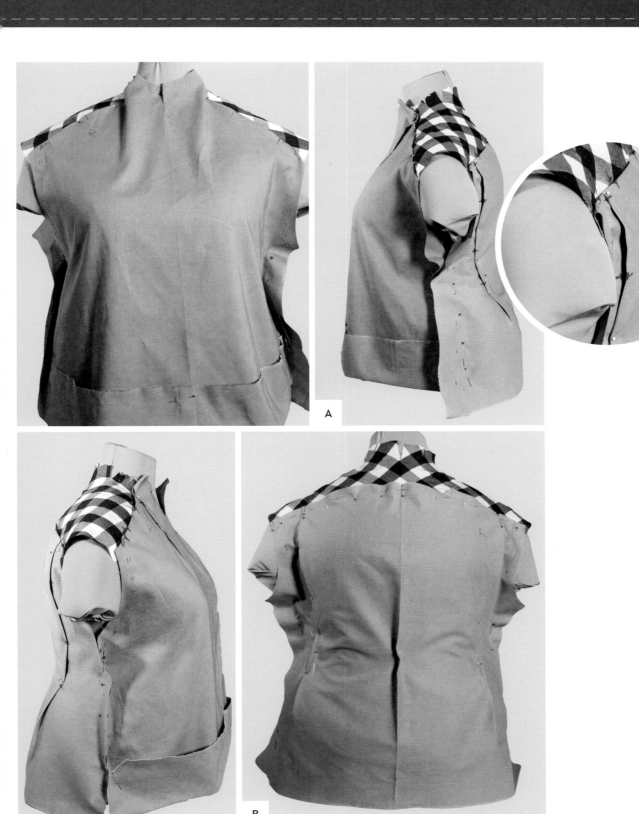

NECKLINE, DARTS, AND PATTERN PREP

Next, it's time to finalize those collar-hidden darts, so I needed to first design the perfect collar. You can trace a collar from another pattern, a source shirt, or drape extra fabric to create your own design. I made a collar mock-up with a straight-edge neckline, and carefully centered and balanced it around the form's neck until I was pleased with the shape of the collar and the garment neckline it established. By folding the collar up, I was able to mark one side of the drape with the new neckline. With the darts and neckline marked, and the collar shape looking good, I was ready to take the front drape off the form to create the front pattern. I folded the drape in half

along the center and around two carbon paper sheets to wheel-trace, with a ruler, pattern lines for both the dart and neckline, including seam allowances. You can see the symmetrical stitching guides for both these details on the unfolded muslin (**A**). Note that I also marked symmetrical armhole curves and front-to-yoke edges, having decided that I could safely cut these, too, on a fold, since the fit didn't appear very different as draped and would be draped again anyway. I need only the top, right half of the front drape going forward. As usual, I included extra-wide seam allowances. Refer to the pdf, "Converting a muslin drape to a paper pattern" for more details.

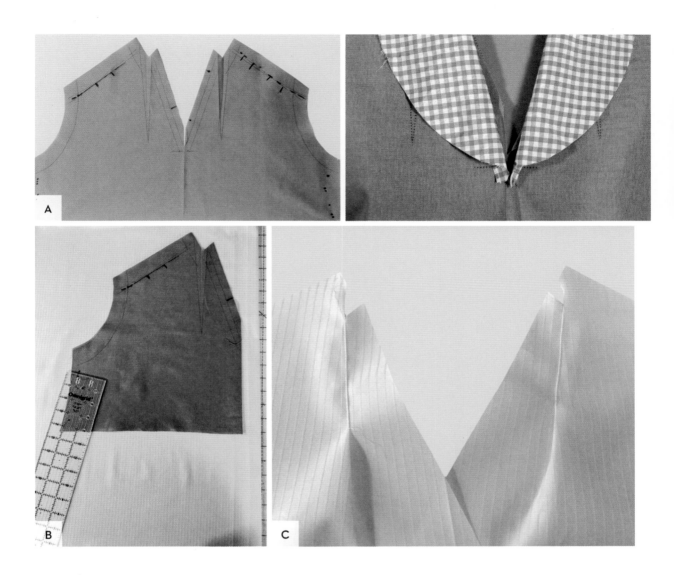

You can see how I used the folded drape to cut out two full-length fashion-fabric fronts (**B**). I added center-front closure seam allowances and extended the side seams with a ruler, aligned to the angle I'd draped earlier at the lower ends of the carbon-marked muslin and again I included wide draping allowances.

I stitched the darts about half way, leaving the rest to press to shape (**C**). I find it's easier to curve these folds inward and more safely out of sight beneath the collar with my iron than by stitching. Perhaps, I should have better shaped the allowances at the dart ends to avoid those deep folds, but at least they fall outside the collar seam line.

REDRAPE THE FRONTS AND BACKS

Now begins the redraping for the front and back. I almost always feel compelled to redrape with new-to-me fabrics and/or a new pattern. The first step, as always, is to position and pin one yoke on the form; and in this case, it will be the inner yoke, wrong side up. I cut the yoke layers on the bias with a center back seam, so the striped patterns of the fashion fabric will mesh nicely when joined to the fronts—something I noticed in an earlier drape.

I've also cut out the back with just enough extra width so I can stitch out the entire vertical center-pinning from yoke to hem to add shape and style to the back. I pin the back to the yoke, matching centers and curves, and proceed to do the ease reductions, carefully and as symmetrically as I can manage, based on marks lightly transferred from the grey muslin drape, shown on page 107. I then lightly mark the seam lines where the back and inner yoke will join later.

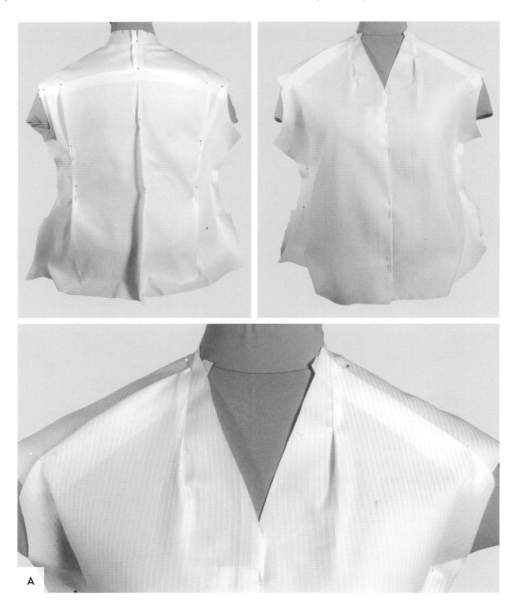

A

The rest of the images record my careful efforts to align the fronts to the inner yoke (**A**, **B**), and then to the outer yoke layer, pinned all together (**C**). Note how helpful it is to be able pin straight into this foam-filled, home-made form (see page 87). I can also bring my iron right up to the form, as needed, to create or remove a crease.

I aligned the folded-under edges of the fronts and outer yoke in much the same way that I butted the cut edges of the woolen yoke and fronts in the previous project (see page 95), and gently pin-marked match points and crease-marked seam lines once the draped pieces looked right. Now, I've got just enough information to take everything off the form, join the fronts as marked to the outer yoke, arrange the yokes right sides together without yet joining the inner layer to the fronts, and then insert the finished collar and neckline facings between them and stitch everything in place together along the neckline. But first, I need to drape the facings.

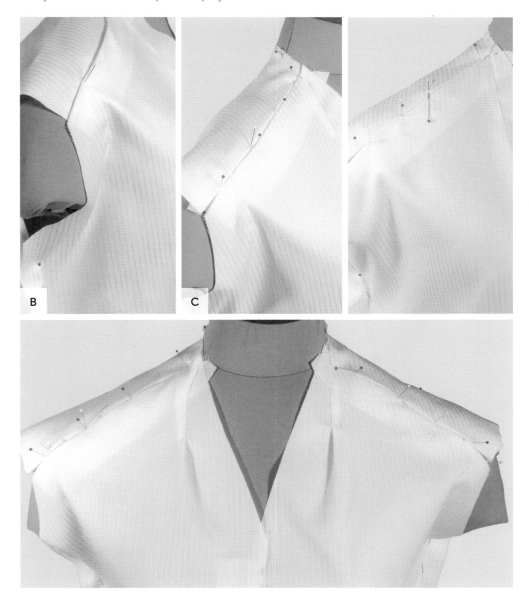

JOIN THE COLLAR BETWEEN THE YOKE LAYERS

Rather than cutting complex one-piece yoke-to-hem facings, I chose to split the facings into simple separate neck and front facings so I could cut them both as on-grain rectangles with the lovely, smooth selvedges of the fabric serving as the edge finish. I started with the neckline rectangles positioned parallel to each front neckline, with the upper ends extended up and under the yoke fronts for about an inch (2.5 cm). I pinned and basted all the layers so the collar was sandwiched between the yoke layers in back, and the right side of the garment and the right side of the facing in front, making sure the collar was right side up on the garment front! I then stitched from the center front of the neckline, all around the neck to the opposite neckline center front. You can see the extended lower end of one neckline facing waiting to be joined to the lower facing (**A**). Unfortunately, once I was finished, I discovered that I hated the oval outer edge shaping I'd cut for the collar. It looked fine in orange gingham on green—and awful white on white it resembled a big platter!

So, off it all came, stitching removed, collar recut, turned and topstitched all over again, and reinserted. And after a well-deserved break, I was ready to add the front facing rectangles and secure the inner yoke front edges, still loose on the inside. But first, before stitching the facings in place, I needed to add the little fabric button loops (**B**). For more details about making fabric button loops and joining the facing pieces, refer to the downloaded pdf, "Construction of the Fitted V-Neck Dress Shirt."

For the front yoke edges, I carefully rearranged the inner yoke layer back into marked place, folding and trimming the front edge so it aligned with the outer yoke's edge, so I can catch both with a single line of edge-stitching from the right side. You can barely see the unfolded inner front seam allowance extending forward in the before detail (inset **A**), and in the after detail (inset **B**), you can now see the edge-stitched outer yoke front with only the single-layer front below it.

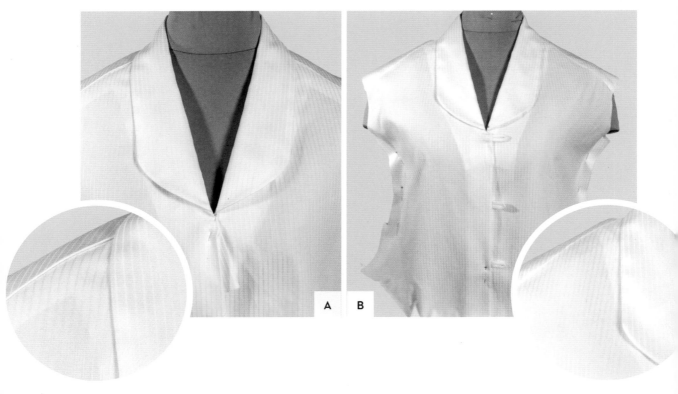

A   B

ADD THE SHIRT BACK BETWEEN THE YOKE LAYERS

As you can see, the upper and lower yokes are nicely aligned in back, ready for me to insert the back (**A**). I've by now decided on, and stitched down, the ease-reduction darts and tucks in the back fabric, so it's ready to go. Notice the wide draping allowances on both the yoke edges and the back edge, now carefully crease-marked on the back and inner yoke following my earlier seam-line markings (page 110), which now need to be trimmed (**A**, **B**).

I am now ready to pin and join the inner yoke to the back with a standard seam along the pressed creases. Once stitched, it's easy to press the edge of the outer yoke carefully over to align with the seam. As this is a curve, I pressed the seam on a tailor's ham (**D**), tacking the edge in place sporadically with glue-stick dabs, and finally topstitching along the fold to finish the seam and hide all the construction bits.

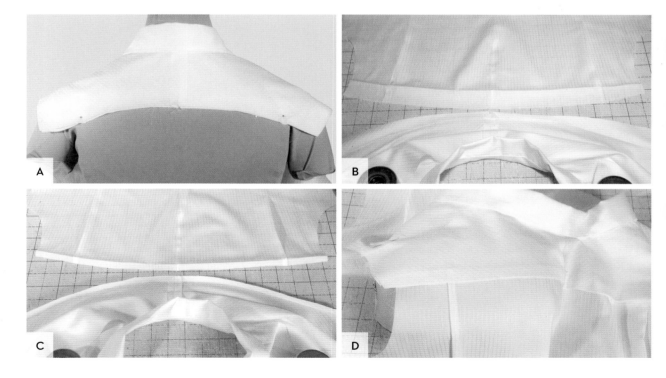

A

B

C

D

ADD THE SLEEVES

There's a slight asymmetry to the armholes, as you can see (**A**), but they appear fine on the form, so I simply mark a uniform ⅜-inch (9 mm) seam allowance all around, using my curve ruler that's perfect for this (see Resources) (**B**). I then cut basic sleeves from the provided medium-tall sleeve cap shapes, choosing the one with a cap-length that matches the length of these armholes, and cutting them with enough cap seam allowance width for a flat-felled seam. For more information see the downloadable pdf, "Flat-Felled Seams." Once the sleeves are cut, it's time to sew the sleeves into closed tubes, and then sew a continuous placket in each sleeve. Don't attach the cuffs yet, but do insert the sleeves into the armhole openings. Refer to the downloadable pdf, Construction for the Fitted V-Neck Dress Shirt."

As I folded under the felling seam al-lowance inside each cap seam line in preparation for the second stitching pass, the distortions from the pins I was using bothered me (**C**), so I tried something I'd not done before: I hand basted the to-be-felled edge onto the armhole (**D**). Except for the little knot near the bottom of the image, I loved how this looked, both the stitches and the seam itself. This was a lovely revelation, recalling the many reports I've read, and generally sniffed at, about the beauties of hand-finished cus-tom shirts, even completely hand-sewn ones. Hand-stitched sleeve seams always come in for special praise, and I finally see why. Machine stitches have a hard look and add stiffness to the multiple layers. So, I ripped out the basting and redid the topstitching by hand all around, as the final finish.

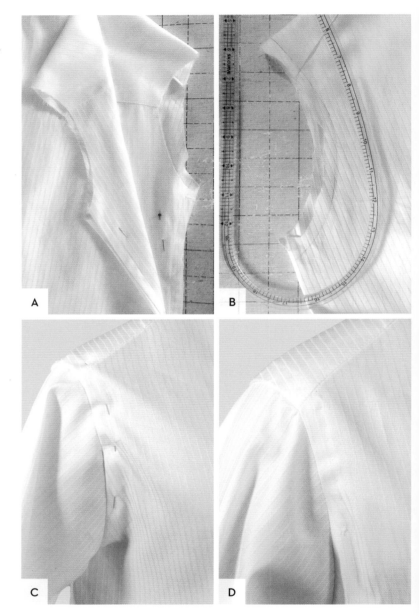

A

B

C

D

FINISH WITH THE HEMS AND CUFFS

The final edge finishing for this dressy shirt involves a lot of folding along straight lines, which demands accuracy and consistency. Here's an easy solution: create custom folding templates, from moderately stiff paper, cut exactly to the shapes you want the final folding to create, then press the hem allowances around them before topstitching. The simple ones I made are shown here.

The cuffs I want for this shirt are narrow, squared off, and soft, so no interfacing; there is no interfacing anywhere in this project. The lovely satin-striped fabric is substantial enough and can easily be further stiffened, if so desired, with a little spray sizing You'll notice I inserted another button loop into each cuff, but otherwise I am making them as described in the downloadable pdf, "Construction of the Fitted V-Neck Dress Shirt." And I always bring out my indispensable, fine-tip forceps to ensure perfect points when turning corners; you'll find detailed directions for this tip in the same pdf.

THE DETAILS

Working with white fabric is always a bit stressful, especially on a project that's as much an ironing odyssey as this one. It is so important to stop and press after each step. I always rely on a tissue-paper press cloth. I use the same light roll-paper for this as for pattern tracing, and kept the iron temperature lower than the cotton setting.

Note the slight curve I nudged into the hidden dart ends at top right (**A**), and the tiny hand-stitched bartack I added to the back of the top-most button loop to fine-tune just where I wanted that button to rest (**B**). Again, the downloadable pdf, "Construction of the Fitted V-Neck Dress Shirt" is a wealth of detailed step-by-step guidance.

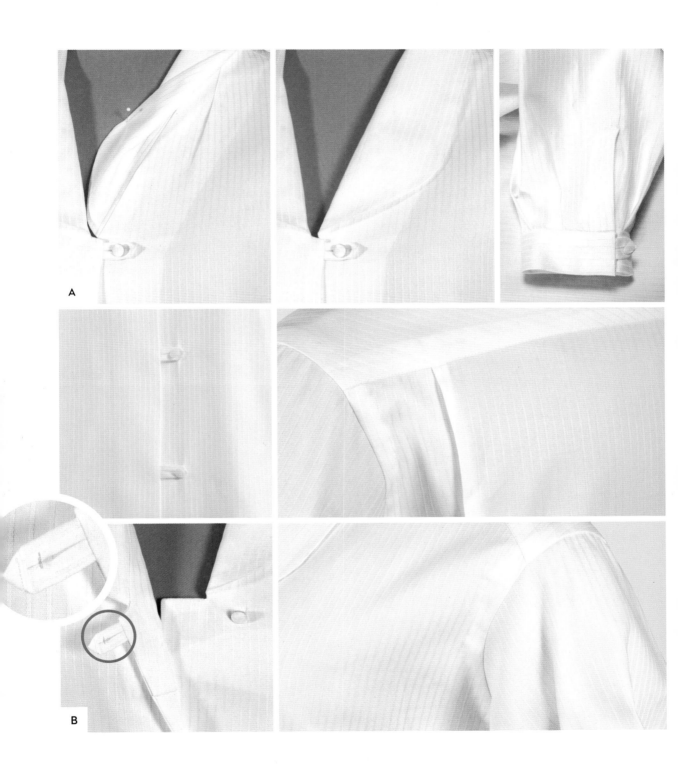

A

B

PROJECT

3

FITTED WRAPPED SHIRTDRESS

All it takes to turn any shirt into a shirtdress is length-ening the hem so it's long enough that the wearer is comfortable wearing it as a dress, not just a top. These shirtdresses (**A**) and (**B**) are typical examples, although the pink one (**C**) is reshaped a little at the sides and below the waist to allow the skirt portion to be form-fitting. The belt makes it hard to tell just how loose it is at the waist, but there's probably some shaping there, too—which is nothing more than what you'd do on the sides of a fitted shirt, starting above the hips and continuing as far down as you'd like.

The remaining examples (**D**), (**E**), and (**F**) clearly represent another simple option: choose a skirt pattern you like and attach it to your chosen shirt with a waistline seam, allowing an abrupt change in total ease.

CONSTRUCTION SEQUENCE

For detailed, how-to construction steps, refer to the downloaded pdf, "Construction of the Fitted Wrapped Shirtdress."

1. Fronts and back joined to outer yoke layer
2. Collar made, then joined to neck between yoke layers and neckline facings and fronts
3. Side seams joined with slit left open for wrap tie
4. Sleeves made and added
5. Wrap ties, vertical edges, and hems finished
6. Button added

More interesting, I think, is to combine either skirt option (straight or full) with a complete restyling of the top, as for this shirtdress (**G**) with the deep V-neckline and wide collar which, becomes a wrap closure at the waist and down the skirt front. Typically, the front closure on any shirtdress extends all the way to the hem, but it doesn't have to. And, the possibilities that different sleeves can add to the redesign of a shirt to a shirtdress are endless.

The wrap shirtdress (**G**), the inspiration for this next project, is where I found and borrowed the collar shape and the wrapped neckline, designed to close at the side waist. I did deplunge it a bit! I also decided that the wrap ties would be visible only in the back, and the front looked better to me falling smoothly without darts (**H**).

I was highly inspired by the fabric, a very fine cotton, that on close inspection revealed a much-minimized version of the striped pattern found on utility fabrics called ticking, and used to be the default covering on equally utility-level mattresses and pillows. This connection, utility fabric with elegant shirtdress, kept drawing me towards a more utility-oriented concept for the project garment, more smock or even apron, than dress.

G

H

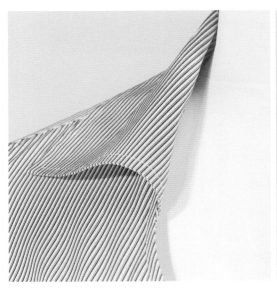

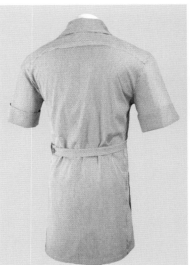

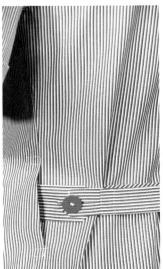

INITIAL DRAPES

To mix as much fitting as possible into a silhouette that I wanted to feel casual and relaxed, I first draped a darted front on form #3, dividing the shaping almost equally above and below the bus (**A**).

I then released the pinned upper darts (**B**). Initially, I expected to retain the lower darts, but after I reshaped the front to create the V-wrapped neckline, constructed a wrapped test muslin, and fiddled with it for a while (of course), I eventually decided that the lower darts could be released, as well (**C**). (Refer to the downloadable pdf for detailed instructions for "Creating a V wrapped neckline from a one-piece front drape."

I also draped a darted back (**D**), but decided to convert the darts to reshaped side seams, by tracing off the pattern with the dart ease pinned out and the drape laid flat as described in chapter 4 (see page 67); this allows me to arrive at the dart-free back muslin (**E**). Before I was sure how I'd eventually handle the wrapped front, I cut a long strip of extra fabric, about 2 inches (5 cm) wide and used it to simulate a variety of belt-tie positions and estimate final lengths. Then I cut out and pin-tested a few sample collar-shape muslins. There is downloadable version of the chosen pattern in the online content, but you can certainly trace a collar from an existing pattern or a source shirt.

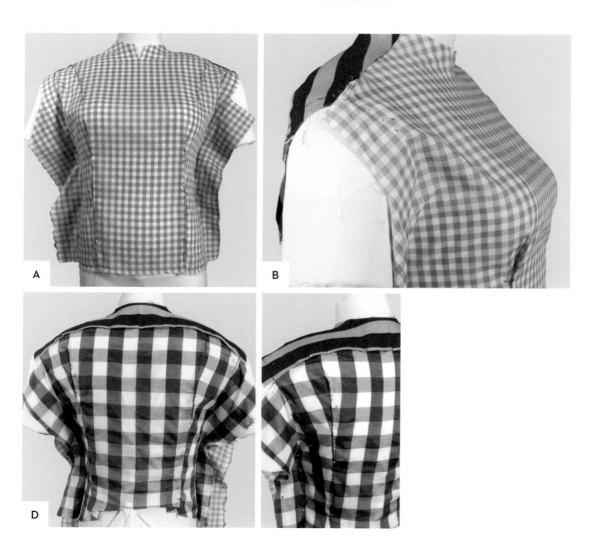

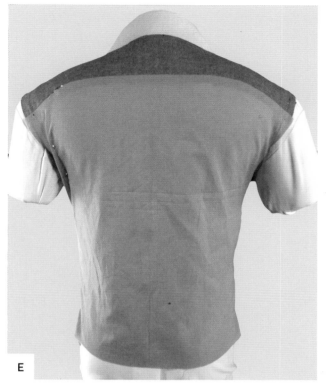

JOIN FRONTS AND BACK TO OUTER YOKE

Satisfied with the shape and design of my wrapping muslin, I used it as the pattern for the fashion fabric, simply extending the straight, vertical side seams as long as necessary to allow a generous hem length, the final length to be determined later. I stitched the outer yoke to the fronts and back, and as you can see (**A**), I found some front-to-yoke tweaking was necessary with the new fabric and the bias-cut neckline, so I removed the stitches from the outer yoke seams I'd overconfidently stitched before checking the pieces in the fashion fabric on the form. I then restitched the front to outer yoke seams to reflect the pinned corrections. I needed at least one yoke layer in place to check and redrape all the other parts and seams, like the front waist-level darts (**B**) I'm still considering, and where to position the collar (**C**).

A

B

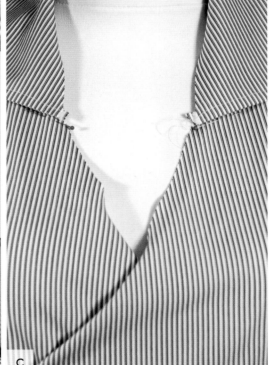

C

ADD THE COLLAR WITH THE INNER YOKE AND BIAS FACING

To attach the basic stitched-and-turned collar, add facings to the rest of the neckline (the yoke finishes the collar seam), and create the outer back waist tie and inner tie, I cut two bias strips for the facings, one of which was long enough to be included as part of the back-waist tie. I then reinforced one edge of each facing with a fusible strip of interfacing (**A**) before stitching the facings to the garment front (beyond the collar). The narrow interfacing helps minimize stretching along the bias neck edges but still allows the facings to easily mold over the many body contours they encounter from neckline to waist. The bias-cut helps prevent the fabric edges from raveling so I won't need to edge finish the facings on this very tight fabric, but if the fabric was a looser weave, I'd have used a bias-cut interfacing and fused it over the full width of the facing. For more detailed instruction, refer to the downloaded pdf, "Construction of the Fitted Wrapped Shirtdress."

You can see how I layered the inner yoke and facing strips, sandwiching the collar in between so the neckline is completely finished by those inner parts (**B**). I then folded under the front and back seam allowances on the inner yoke to match the existing seams for the outer yoke. These edges were carefully glue-stick basted in place on the inside, then secured by edge-stitching the upper yoke from the garment right side, just as in the previous project (see page 112).

A

B

ADD SLEEVES, TIES, AND HEM

Next, I stitched the side seams with hand-folded, flat-felled seams, leaving a roughly 3-inch (2.5 cm) waist-level break in the stitching on the left side seam for the inner wrap tie. I can easily shorten the gap in the stitching after seeing exactly how the inner tie extension fits through the opening.

With the sides closed, I made sleeve muslins using the medium-tall sleeve cap shape from the provided pattern collection, measured to fit the armholes. With the sleeves slipped onto the form and into the armhole openings, I was able to simultaneously find the final seam lines I'd use for both the armholes and the sleeves (**A**, **B**). I then used each marked test sleeve as the pattern to cut right and left, custom-draped sleeves from the fashion fabric, and inserted these as tubes, into the already closed, also custom-draped armholes.

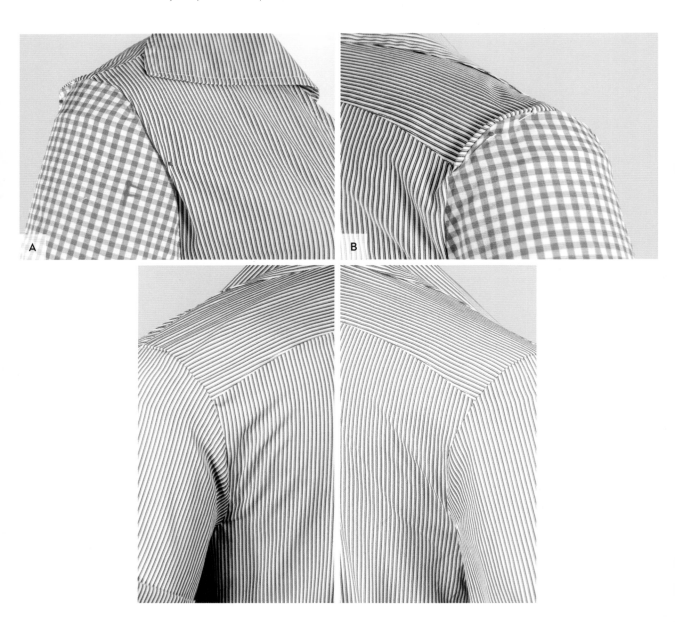

A few distinctive and precisely made finishing details would be, I thought, sufficient to lift this very simple garment into something a little special. You'll find detailed descriptions for everything shown here in the online material for this project, but here are the highlights.

I first made the short inner-wrap tie (**A**) from two pre-folded fabric layers simply edge-stitched together (**B**, **C**), and then joined this to the inner wrap edge with a top-stitched patch (**D**).

The longer neckline facing strip also faces the back wrap-tie, which is joined to the edge of the overlapping waist layer, so I arranged its bias-oriented stripes to peek out slightly above the outer wrap-tie layer, forming a sort of faux-piping (**E**).

And as you can see (**F**), I continued to exercise my fondness for folded buttonhole strips by adding one to the end of this more visible of the two wrap ties.

And, a double-fold machine stitched hem is the way to finish (**G**).

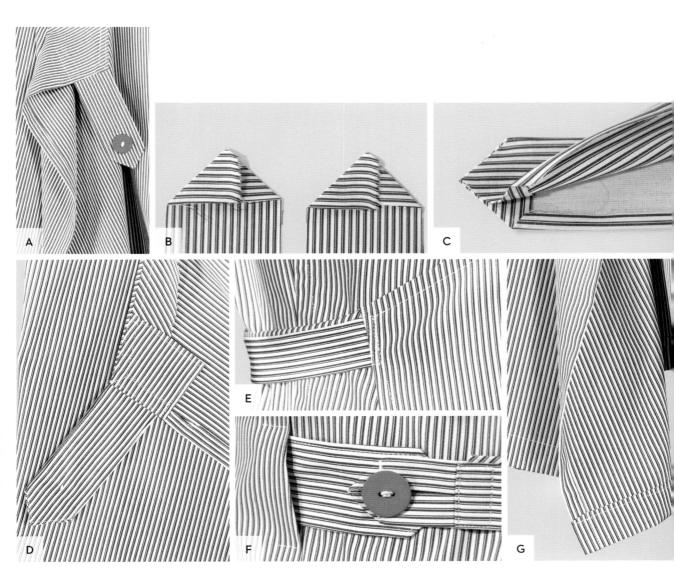

PROJECT
4

TIGHT DENIM WESTERN SHIRT

This was the one project that I had in mind to include in this book from the beginning, an obviously classic design, well-suited to a tight fit, and with many details I looked forward to exploring. The basic pattern came directly from the last test muslin developed in chapter 5 on form #4, the athletic male form, used at top far right on which to also evaluate the placement and shapes of the pockets, flaps, and Western yokes, initially drawn on pattern paper and tested here with muslin scraps.

CONSTRUCTION SEQUENCE

For detailed, how-to construction steps, refer to downloaded pdf, "Construction of the "Tight Denim Western Shirt."

This shirt is constructed in much the same order as shown on page 88, with sleeves added as tubes.

1. Add details to fronts
2. Join back, then fronts to yoke layers
3. Make and add collar on stand
4. Add sleeve plackets, close underarm seam, and add cuffs
5. Close side seams
6. Insert sleeves
7. Finish hems and add snaps

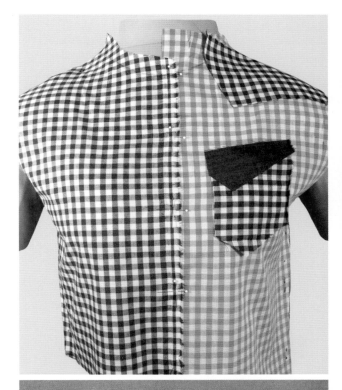

Once I'm happy with each front detail shape, after having made a few slight design changes, I redraw the patterns, trace them onto manila-folder-weight paper to create custom folding templates, like for project 2 (see page 115). These templates, cut to the exact shape of the final, finished pieces, ensure the folding under of seam allowances accurately and symmetrically. The heavier paper reflects the heavier denim fabric used for this project. As usual, I use ironed-down glue from a glue stick to secure the pressed edges.

Templates also offer an easy way to line the pocket flaps: Just fold each layer (denim upper layer and contrast lining layer) around the same template separately (**A**), and join them right sides out with topstitching, instead of trying to perfectly turn all six points, which would be difficult). I use the same pressing-template process for the front yokes (**B**) and for each pocket, including the upper hemmed opening edge.

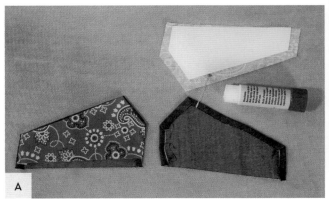

A

B

ASSEMBLING THE SHIRT FRONT

Once I'd cut the denim front, back, and yoke from the pattern from chapter 5, I assembled the pieces into testable shape, with front bands completed, and fronts and back joined to the yoke layers (the outer yoke not yet secured in front, to allow for placing and catching the add-on Western front yokes). I then discovered that, despite all my efforts to eliminate any darts at the chest, this heavier, stiff fabric insisted on folding into the inarguable armhole darts that are apparent in the close-ups below.

I simply pressed the dart folds down into actual darts to be dealt with later, and carried on with the final placement and marking for all those template-formed details, a long, painstaking process for which measuring tools were mostly unhelpful, given the slightly asymmetrical shoulders. Placement was all done by eye, and with so many microshifts and repinnings my chalk placement marks barely held and were mostly replaced with last-minute pins before they disappeared altogether.

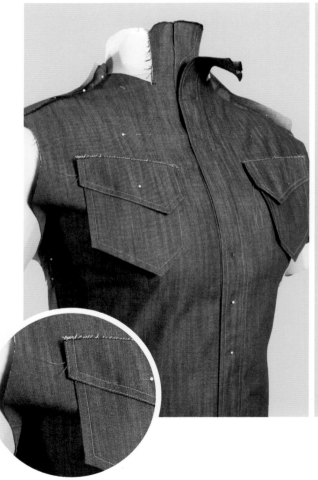

The oddly extended fabric at the neckline center was also added at the hem (where it's more useful than at the neck). It's there to allow extra front band length to manipulate the collar placement and finish the rolled hem. The neckline extensions were a momentary whim, but the extra length did help with handling during the finishing steps.

Note that the finished, but as yet only pinned-on, pockets are only topstitched at this stage, leaving the edge-stitching until the pockets are stitched in place on the shirt front (after the darts are stitched!). I left the front-yoke edges unstitched because they didn't have wide enough seam allowances to be caught in the topstitching and would need to be edge-stitched down first. All these details are explained step-by-step in the downloadable pdf, "Construction of the Tight Denim Western Shirt."

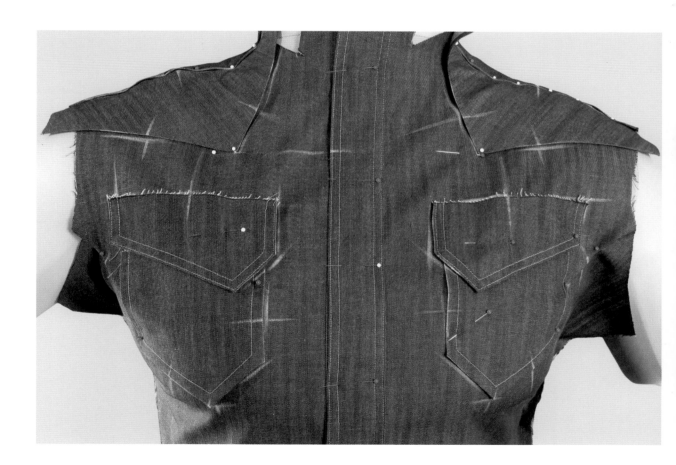

MAKE THE COLLAR

As usual, I draped a custom neck line with a ring of paper dropped, fitted, and then marked along the bottom edge onto the drape.

Follow these steps to easily create sharp, symmetrical points for the collar, just as I described earlier for the collar in the shirt-jacket project, but didn't as completely document.

1 Cut appropriate interfacing to the exact finished shape of the collar's outer edges so it extends into a seam allowance only at the edge that will be joined to the collar stand.

2 Fuse or baste (here, it's fused) the interfacing to the outer collar, which is cut with enough folding allowance to make double folds that wrap around and over the interfacing and the inner collar layers, covering the edges.

3 Cut the under-collar layer a little smaller than the outer collar and so that it follows the interfacing edge closely (**A**). Trim off the points on both the collar layers to reduce bulk (**B**).

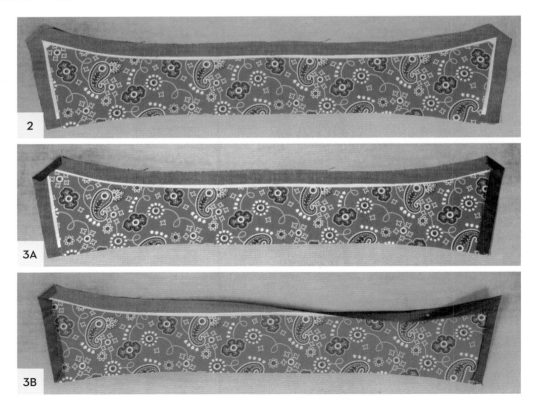

Follow the folding progression, as shown, using liberal glue basting and an iron. Carefully done, this process is the best path to really sharp, matching points (**A**) on less-than-square corners that I've ever found. I like the wrapped-edge effect as well.

My first test sample, with the pink inner layer (**B**), is shown both to encourage you to make at least one test sample and to point out a subtle detail. The garment collar above it shows how I wrapped the long collar edge after the short edges, while on the test sample I did the ends last, not noticing until too late that this order results in a miter that's easier to catch securely with topstitching.

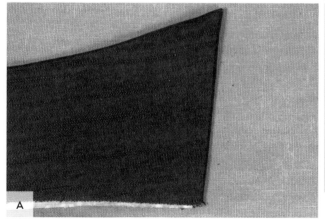

A

B

ADDING THE COLLAR AND CUFFS

To further prepare the collar for joining to the collar stand, I pressed its remaining unfinished edge to the wrong side, forcing the fold to follow the curve of the original collar pattern (**A**).

I machine basted along this fold using a zipper foot to get as close to the fold as possible without hitting it (**B**). This step holds in the excess length forced onto the outer collar, compared to the inner layers from the previous step, which I find makes for a smooth collar fold when worn. I then trim this seam allowance back to ¼ inch (6 mm) after basting so it's easier to match the stand seam allowance, also ¼ inch (6 mm).

The other images show the steps I took to join the collar to the collar stand, which I'd previous attached to the neckline using a technique described in detail in my first shirtmaking book and the downloadable pdf, "Construction of the Tight Denim Western Shirt." In short, it leaves the stand's top edge open, ready to be joined to the prepared collar in just the same way as in the white-shirt project for joining cuffs to sleeves (see page 115). With the collar-insertion version, the stand is treated like a cuff, and the collar like a sleeve, with all the collar layers attached to one side only of the stand with the first right-sides-together seam. This leaves the remaining stand edge to be folded under (**C**) and caught with

topstitching from the other side after you've tucked the collar allowances neatly inside the stand opening. The remaining images (**D**, **E**) show how to make the stitches of the first seam smoothly blend into the curve of the stand where the seam stops.

The remaining details show the cuffs arranged and pinned for stitching as described for the collar. Notice how the pinning can arranged to both hold the cuffs in place and the inner cuff layer out of the way of the subsequent stitching at the same time.

ADDING THE SLEEVES

Because I always choose relatively loose-fitting shirts when I make my own, I've never considered, nor even tested, the commonly repeated idea that shirt-sleeve caps should, like those of other set-in sleeve types, be at least slightly gathered or eased at the yoke edge before insertion. It's always been obvious to me that this extra step is neither required for comfort nor needed for a smooth finish on my own projects, nor does it appear to have been done on any of my collected custom and ready-to-wear, mostly men's, shirts.

For this tight-fitting project, I thought a slightly gathered sleeve cap might be worth trying, given the additional tension such a close fit subjects to every piece in the garment. So, this is what I've done for the three images below. My verdict ("Bah!") is, I hope, understandable.

Unless I misunderstand how a gathered shirt-sleeve cap is to be done—and that's certainly possible—it's a clearly a mess. In the meantime, I'll persist in ignoring this insertion method unless I'm working with fabric that can be iron-shrunk to make this sort of ease work more gracefully.

The tight fit does make draping a test sleeve in an armhole more difficult than with looser fits. After several failed attempts to position, adjust, and secure a measured cap to these draped armholes using just fingers and pins, I finally found a baste-on-the-form method that both drew the edges more snugly together as I stitched and very securely held all in place. I even liked the look, in a sort of frontierish way, and have filed away the idea of using it as a finish on future shirt-like projects.

The images show how I the basted sleeve into the armhole, well pressed to smooth out the stitches, which were only applied to the top half of the armhole, since I couldn't reach the underam area. The sleeves are now ready for machine stitching, or basting (to the inside of the stitches already there).

Note how the last image at right demonstrates the unpredictable, unmeasureable, but easily drapable, unique and varying seam lines that such a careful fitting can result in, on cap and armhole simultaneously.

Here, you can see my results after machine stitching the sleeves into place. Note that I've treated each side differently—this is a shirt for a fictional body after all—pressing the allowances out, in towards the body in the usual way (**A**) on the form's right shoulder, and towards the sleeve (**B**) on the form's left shoulder, just to see the differences. Subtle, to be sure, but clearly smoother when pressed out. Note the hand basting on the pressed-in side (lesson learned!) in preparation for the machine flat-felling to come.

You'll also note the slight puckering along the seam that persists at the top of each sleeve. No doubt this is the problem cap easing is meant to solve, if I could only see how with nonshrinkable fabrics. It is, however, possible to carefully hand-stitch much of this away, pulling the slight excess lengths in from the wrong side, before going any further with seam finishing. If you're willing to put in the effort . . .

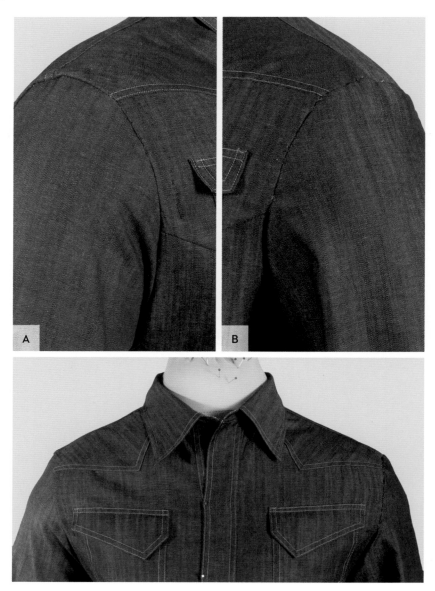

STITCHING THE HEM

Here's how I formed the hems, again slightly differently on each side, for comparison's sake. Each edge was hand-folded twice, with glue-stick and iron in hand, on a padded surface so pins could help, just as described for princess-seam prep (see page 83). After thorough pressing, they were top- and edge-stitched as everywhere else on the shirt, with the front band ends out of the way, and then folded over these stitches and edge-stitched down symmetrically (lots of options are possible here) to provide a smoother and more interesting finish compared to trying to catch all their bulk in the hem roll (**A**), (**C**).

The little gusset attached on the other side depends on the hem curves blending into the side seam rather than across it, which requires that one of the side-seam allowances is clipped to roll the other way at the hem, which the gusset can neatly cover when it's topstitched in place from the right side (**B**). The gusset itself is a turned triangle shape, folded at the bottom and left open at the top point, and then poked into the turned shape with the tip of my forceps, which nicely curve the stitched sides, as needed, to match the hem curves.

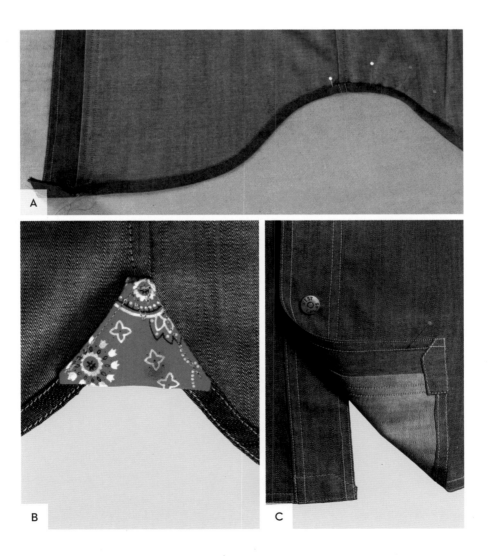

A

B

C

FINISHING DETAILS

The snap closures are, of course, the expected closure on a shirt like this, a bit hair-raising to install, but easier than buttons and buttonholes. I just couldn't bring myself to do that to the collar stand ends—so I didn't.

I hope something in all this will prove helpful in your shirt-making journeys. Let me know if any questions come up. I'm sure to have an opinion!

RESOURCES

Clickable links for all these resources, and many more, can be found online at my Pinterest site (Shirtmaking with DPC) and my website (**www.shirtmakingwithdpc.com**).

SHIRT CONSTRUCTION

My previous books and videos on shirtmaking are available wherever books and videos are sold. The first, *Shirtmaking*, covers the construction of a classic dress shirt in great detail and only turning to other styles briefly in the final chapter. The specific techniques I developed for this book are shown in the DVD *Shirtmaking Techniques*, both from The Taunton Press.

The Shirtmaking Workbook, from Creative Publishing International, covers—and provides many full-size downloadable patterns—the details for a wide range of shirt styles, from dress and sport to knit and folk shirts, including shirt jackets. Extensive construction details are also offered as downloadable pdf documents. Many of these techniques and a few patterns are also available in my Craftsy class "**Shirtmaking Details: Beyond the Basics**." Neither of these resources cover fitting, however. Other Craftsy classes pertinent to the topics in this book include "**The Classic Tailored Shirt**," by Pam Howard, "**Sew Better, Sew Faster, Shirtmaking**," by Janet Pray, and "**Customize Your Dress Form**," by Judy Jackson. There are many other pattern-fitting classes at Craftsy, but none to-date cover draping to fit.

There are of course many mostly free online resources on all aspects of shirtmaking, although again, none that I know of on draping to fit. An excellent collection of these is at **www.curvysewingcollective.com/round-up-of-shirt-making-technique-resources-online**

DRAPING AND PATTERNMAKING TOOLS AND SUPPLIES

The **gingham** and **solid fabrics** I used for all the draping demonstrations shown in this book were bought from **www.fabric.com**. Search for Richcheck Gingham, and Premium Broadcloth to locate the exact items.

I always prefer poly/cotton-blend 60" (152 cm) wide ginghams for initial draping tests, typically tearing off a 20" or 24" (50 or 60 cm) length across the entire width of the unwashed, pressed yardage for each project, from which I've been able to cut both front and back draping rectangles for all the forms shown in this book. I bought several colors of the all-cotton 42" (107 cm) Premium Broadcloth for construction demos, but I found it to be good for crisp-fabric draping tests as well, as it has virtually no stretch. I don't wash this stuff either. There's nothing special about either fabric, but they're easy to find and well-priced, plus occasionally on sale at a good discount. My wide-striped blue and taupe yoke fabric is an upholstery-weight cotton I've had around forever.

My preferred **pattern papers** include 27" x 34" (70 x 85 cm) *Easel Pads* for medium-weight durability, a useful size and easy storage without rolling, which I mostly use for garment pin-tracing and detail drafting of large pattern pieces for specific designs. For smaller pieces, easy pencil-tracing, and less-durable needs, I also keep on hand a roll of translucent, inexpensive 21"-wide (53 cm) *Medical Pattern Paper*. Both italicized names are good search terms at online retailers.

Saral brand washable tracing carbon works well and comes in rolls and various colors for large projects. I wish I had a good source for large waxed-carbon sheets.

Ordinary **poster** and **foam-core boards** are easier to buy as single sheets locally. Online, I find them usually sold in packs, which can be expensive if in a wider range of sizes. The poster board is for cutting out precise pressing templates (manila file folders work well, too). Foam core is for sliding underneath the top easel-pad sheet when pin-tracing, although corrugated cardboard can work as well in a pinch. Tape two small foam-core sheets together if necessary to get complete coverage.

I depend on several colors and sizes of **permanent marker**, such as Sharpie brand, my usual choice. The fat ones are perfect for bleed-through marking on double fabric layers, the thin ones are better for precision permanent drawing on fabric or paper, although I usually prefer ordinary graphite pencils for paper.

My favorite **curved rulers** and **measuring wheels** come from **SA Curve**. Go online and search at www.etsy.com for SA Curve or LunaGrafixCo.

ACKNOWLEDGEMENTS

Many thanks to the great crew at the Quarto Group for all their usual good cheer and excellent work and especially to my editor, Beth Baumgartel, whose many pointed questions helped immeasurably to tighten up my text. Her work was invaluable—all my readers should join in with my gratitude!

ABOUT THE AUTHOR

David Page Coffin's career as a sewing expert, teacher, and writer began with a self-published how-to book about making custom shirts, which became a bestseller and led to an 18-year editor's post at *Threads* magazine, where both his sewing and publishing skills found a worldwide audience. Coffin is also the author/creator of the authoritative and best-selling sewing books *Making Trousers for Men & Women* and *The Shirtmaking Workbook*, hundreds of sewing articles, two Craftsy classes, and YouTube videos with hundreds of thousands of views. He has taught workshops throughout the United States, Canada, and in the UK, appeared on nationally syndicated sewing shows, and been a featured host on various sewing bulletin boards and websites. He lives in Brookings, Oregon, with his wife Ellen. www.shirtmakingwithdpc.com

INDEX